The Way of the Awakened

by Darcy Cleome

Copyright © 2014 by Darcy Cleome

Published and distributed in the United States
by: Violet Flame Publishing,
www.violetflamepublishing.com

All rights reserved. No part of this book may be reproduced by any mechanical, photographic, or electronic process, or in the form of a photographic recording; nor may it be stored in a retrieval system, transmitted, or otherwise be copied for public or private use—other than for "fair use" as brief quotations embodied in articles and reviews without prior written permission of the publisher.

The author of this book does not dispense medical advice or prescribe the use of any technique as a form of treatment for physical, emotional, or medical problems without the advice of a physician, either directly or indirectly. The intent of the author is only to offer information of a general nature to help you, the reader, in your quest for emotional and Spiritual well being. In the event you use any of the information in this book for yourself, which is your constitutional right, the author and the publisher assume no responsibility for your actions.

Library of Congress Control Number: 2014914303!
ISBN# 978-0-9899985-0-5
1st edition: July 2014

Dedication

To the Awakened, who blazed trails before us;
to the Souls who travel the way of the healer;
to all those in service to Mother Earth; and
to the 'shiny' children of our future.

Acknowledgments

When I began writing this book, I had no idea the effort the process would take or rewards it would provide. Today, I can say that it takes commitment, perseverance and, most of all, a belief in the content. It has given me new understanding, confirmed concepts that I believe in, and has enhanced my appreciation for life's experiences.

My grandmother and namesake, Cleome Fleischmann, never feared speaking her truth. She gave me the gift of intuitive insight, and taught me to accept responsibility for this gift. My mother, who was my biggest fan, always told me I could do and be anything my heart desired. In the writing of this book, I realized she also nourished and encouraged my ability to imagine. When I encountered challenges, these gifts were instrumental in my personal growth and advancement. Both my grandmother and my mother have my love and appreciation.

My children's gifts to me have been as teachers and mirrors. Weston is a good listener and has the capacity to be present in the moment. He is naturally empathic and really 'gets' me. Trenton has inspired me with his 'no fear' approach to life. He takes any situation and makes it an adventure. They are true blessings. My cousin Lindy, who is like a sister to me, had the courage to stand by my side, even when the work I did made her uncomfortable.

My students and clients are my teachers and continual source of inspiration. The Amethyst Healing Center collective members are part of my inner circle, and together we create a network of support and motivation for each other.

A special thanks to Sheila Garcia, who shared a year of Wednesdays to write with me. I would not have started this project without her dedication. I also want to thank Sheila's husband, Chuck, who made sure we ate. Michele Roest took the time to read the manuscript and perform the final edit, giving precious feedback. I enjoyed our serendipitous and magical meetings. Nancy McKarney helped me with the book cover and logo.

Last, but certainly not least, I express my gratitude and thankfulness to Source, and My Team of Spirit Guides, Angels and Ascended Master Teachers. I especially appreciate Master Saint Germain who keeps the violet flame aglow. I hope that I was able to capture and communicate their immense wisdom in this book. May I always remain their student, and keep an open-minded state of awe and excitement for traversing The Way.

TABLE OF CONTENTS

Introduction 1

PART ONE
The Phenomenon..3

CHAPTER ONE
Awakening..5

CHAPTER TWO
The Fall..13

CHAPTER THREE
The Surrender..19

CHAPTER FOUR
The Gleaning..27

CHAPTER FIVE
Healing..35

PART TWO
The Transformation..47

CHAPTER SIX
Soul Examination...49

CHAPTER SEVEN
Multidimensional Healing..57

CHAPTER EIGHT
Energetic Pathways..69

CHAPTER NINE
Resetting Our Karmic Clocks 81

PART THREE
The Way..93

CHAPTER TEN
Uncovering Our Authentic Selves 95

CHAPTER ELEVEN
Spirit Guides, Angels & Ascended Master Teachers 105
CHAPTER TWELVE
The Way Seers..119
CHAPTER THIRTEEN
Service to Spirit 133
CHAPTER FOURTEEN
Creating The Life We Desire..141

Other Titles by The Author 155

About The Author..157

Recommended Reading..161

Introduction

This is *my* story. The information in this book is Truth according to my level of consciousness and insight at this time. I invite you to take from it what feels right to you, at the soul level.

This book contains the essence of the philosophy I believe in and live by. I use these collective tenets in my private practice with students and clients. I was encouraged to share them, and have done so with the hope that others could identify with and be motivated by them. The body of this work is universal in its meaning. I hope it gives you, the reader, valuable insights as a soul having a human experience.

It has been my honor to channel, heal, teach and now write with my Spirit Guides, Angels and Ascended Master Teachers. My journey has been an amazing adventure, a challenge, and a continual awakening. Through my relationship with these spirit beings and the work of applying their ancient wisdom, I have witnessed astonishing life changes in myself and others. I have come to know that we are vast beings of energy in the form of light, frequency and consciousness. Many people are awakening to who they are at the soul level. My intention for this book is that it will give readers insightful tools for their spiritual tool belts, empowering them on their journey.

The Way of the Awakened is organized in three parts. Part One, *The Phenomenon*, describes my personal journey, which began with a near-death experience during the birth of my first son. It proceeds through my process of exploring and developing my healing potential, and ends with my current life as a multidimensional healer. I have shared these experiences in the hopes that they will provide comfort and inspiration to others on their healing path.

Part Two, *The Transformation*, begins with soul examination and multidimensional healing. We explore energetic pathways that are common to many healing modalities. This section also includes information on how to become aware of and release negative life patterns and reset our karmic clocks.

Part Three, *The Way*, chronicles experiences that expanded my capabilities as a multidimensional healer. It offers a series of suggestions on how others can uncover their authentic selves. I have included a description of the Spirit Guides, Angels and Ascended Master Teachers that I work with. In this section I delve into our psychic abilities and discuss way seers. In my opinion, full actualization of our psychic and intuitive skills can only be achieved through a commitment of service to Spirit. Everyone has the potential to create the life they desire by practicing *The Way of the Awakened*.

Introduction

This is *my* story. The information in this book is Truth according to my level of consciousness and insight at this time. I invite you to take from it what feels right to you, at the soul level.

This book contains the essence of the philosophy I believe in and live by. I use these collective tenets in my private practice with students and clients. I was encouraged to share them, and have done so with the hope that others could identify with and be motivated by them. The body of this work is universal in its meaning. I hope it gives you, the reader, valuable insights as a soul having a human experience.

It has been my honor to channel, heal, teach and now write with my Spirit Guides, Angels and Ascended Master Teachers. My journey has been an amazing adventure, a challenge, and a continual awakening. Through my relationship with these spirit beings and the work of applying their ancient wisdom, I have witnessed astonishing life changes in myself and others. I have come to know that we are vast beings of energy in the form of light, frequency and consciousness. Many people are awakening to who they are at the soul level. My intention for this book is that it will give readers insightful tools for their spiritual tool belts, empowering them on their journey.

The Way of the Awakened is organized in three parts. Part One, *The Phenomenon*, describes my personal journey, which began with a near-death experience during the birth of my first son. It proceeds through my process of exploring and developing my healing potential, and ends with my current life as a multidimensional healer. I have shared these experiences in the hopes that they will provide comfort and inspiration to others on their healing path.

Part Two, *The Transformation*, begins with soul examination and multidimensional healing. We explore energetic pathways that are common to many healing modalities. This section also includes information on how to become aware of and release negative life patterns and reset our karmic clocks.

Part Three, *The Way*, chronicles experiences that expanded my capabilities as a multidimensional healer. It offers a series of suggestions on how others can uncover their authentic selves. I have included a description of the Spirit Guides, Angels and Ascended Master Teachers that I work with. In this section I delve into our psychic abilities and discuss way seers. In my opinion, full actualization of our psychic and intuitive skills can only be achieved through a commitment of service to Spirit. Everyone has the potential to create the life they desire by practicing *The Way of the Awakened*.

PART ONE

The Phenomenon

Phenomenon: 1. A significant and rare occurrence that is visible or directly observable as an appearance, action, change or event. 2. A consciousness, apprehended by the mind, in opposition to that which is believed to exist. 3. The metaphysical opinion that these realities are that which the human mind can have no knowledge.

PART ONE

The Phenomenon

Phenomenon: *1. A significant and rare occurrence that is visible or directly observable as an appearance, action, change or event. 2. A consciousness, apprehended by the mind, in opposition to that which is believed to exist. 3. The metaphysical opinion that these realities are that which the human mind can have no knowledge.*

CHAPTER ONE

Awakening

"Some wake up gradually through a series of 'A-ha' moments, some have always known, and some are jarred awake by a life altering event. The latter, my dear, is you!"
~Master Saint Germain

People ask me, "What do you do here?" By 'here,' they are referring to Amethyst Healing Center, the collective of healing practitioners I founded.

My usual response is, "We do many forms of alternative healing, including acupuncture, massage, intuitive reading, astrology and energy medicine." During this initial encounter with someone, I try to discern what I can say that will create a bridge for us to connect. Many times, this is their first encounter with alternative healing, and I feel like a tour guide, responsible for the success of their trip. My job is to find the words that will reach them at the soul level, where their truth resides.

Sometime during our initial encounter, the significance of our exchange is intuitively revealed to me. The possibilities include a potential client who needs or seeks healing work, a student who wishes to develop their own abilities, or just a fertile soul in which to plant the seed of awareness and curiosity. I may not be the gardener, watering and tending the seed, nor will I get to see the bloom, although those moments do happen in my work. Regardless of their initial intentions, I have found that those who are drawn here are looking for understanding and knowledge.

Language is a gift. It makes us, as humans, unique. Many times someone has walked away from a first time meeting with the statement, "I am not sure what it is you said, but it rings true for me." A few timely words can open a door to new awareness. I have witnessed this process in my own life and the lives of many of my clients.

The next question I am often asked is how I came to develop my intuitive and healing abilities. In my case I was jarred awake by a life-altering event. Here is the story of how my own awakening began.

As a girl, I was heavily influenced by my mother's hopes for me. She wanted me to have all the opportunities that she had missed out on in her life. She always told me I could do or be anything I wanted. Growing up, I attended a collection of schools, including Baptist, Lutheran, First Christian and Catholic. I was a member of Job's Daughters, a Masonic youth organization for girls. I received classes in good behavior, etiquette, and modeling. Yes, I even learned to balance a book on my head! Early work included modeling for department store designers and buyers. I also participated in fashion shows and pageants. I competed for and won the title of San Fernando Valley DeMolay League Sweetheart and along the way, I met Todd, the man who would become my husband. He was a prominent member of DeMolay International, a Masonic youth organization for young men. I was seventeen years old when I became engaged, and married by the age of eighteen. I went from being my mother's daughter to becoming my husband's wife.

The year I turned twenty-two, I had a near-death, out-of-body experience that changed the course my life. I had been in a stable marriage for almost five years, and had started working at an exciting job with the Department of Defense that carried lots of responsibility. We had completed construction on our beautiful new home. I was just developing myself as an individual, and starting to spread my wings as an adult. Around this time, my husband discussed with me his desire to start a family, and I agreed. I just did not expect it to happen so quickly!

My first feelings about discovering I was pregnant were mixed. I was excited, scared and disappointed at the same time. It would be simple to say that the skydiving trip I had planned (and now cancelled) was the main cause of my disappointment, but as I have learned, nothing is ever quite that simple, or as it seems. While I was excited about becoming a mother, I also felt that I hadn't had a chance to fully savor the sense of freedom and independence of that phase of my life. This new person growing inside me would require my total attention and care, and its survival depended upon my ability to give it all that it needed. It meant that my personal dreams would have to be put on hold. I kept these feelings to myself and prepared for the stages of pregnancy and childbirth by learning everything I could.

When physical complications arose in my pregnancy, I realized I needed to put my own health first in order to take care of my baby. My blood pressure was dangerously high, which forced me to curtail some of the activities I enjoyed. There were concerns that I might give birth prematurely. I lived a one and a half hour drive from the hospital's neonatal facility and was placed in the hospital on bed rest until my condition stabilized. Separated from family and friends, dealing with the noisy, hectic pace of the hospital, I was very frustrated. I did have a private room next to the nurse's station and the highlighted memory of this time was when the nurses joined me in my room to watch the first televised episode of 'Oprah.'

After three weeks in the hospital, I was pleased find out that I might get to go home the next day. That night, I woke up with a stomachache. Not wanting to ruin my chances of going home, I imagined that it was something minor. But around 3:30 a.m., I gave up and called the nurse. She took my blood pressure, was obviously concerned with my condition, and insisted that my doctor be called.

The doctor arrived at 5:00 a.m., and informed me that my body was not clearing the baby's waste properly. Toxicity had developed and eclampsia was threatening both our lives. My husband was called and advised that he needed to leave for the hospital immediately. My condition had become so serious, they told him I might not make it.

The doctor began administering medication through my intravenous tube. A side effect of the drug was the feeling of heat rushing through my body, and I was instructed to squeeze his hand if it became too intense. My last memory was squeezing as hard as I could.

The next thing I was aware of was the sensation of floating above a hospital room. I seemed to be suspended high enough to see into other rooms and had a sense of what was happening. I felt very detached from the activity below and did not identify with what was going on there. My attention was more on marveling at the view. In fact, emotions were fairly absent. It was as if I was watching a movie.

I realized I could see through normally solid objects, including walls and people. There was some color, but denser objects seemed darker. The light came predominately from the people. They were lit from within, by a light located at approximately heart level. The intensity appeared much brighter than the electric light fixtures and flickered like firelight.

As I became more aware of my immediate surroundings, I noticed that I was also able to see into the floors above me. My vision was panoramic, with the added ability to see through things. Of the five physical senses, it seemed that I could see and hear. I do not know if I could actually feel, but I had an internal awareness that was like the feeling of floating.

Suddenly, I noticed an orb of light rapidly approaching, leaving a trail of light behind. As it came in front of me, it paused. A face appeared within its glow and locked eyes with me briefly, showing curiosity and interest. I turned to watch it leave, and it was then that I saw other beings like me, suspended as I was. Some had full body figures, while others seemed like fragments. We all seemed to be independent observers of the activity around us. I felt a profound acceptance of all that I witnessed.

Noise and activity brought my attention back to the room below me. I noticed small details such as the door to the room, which had a thick, rope-like layer of dust on top of it. If I had to describe my emotional state, it was as if I was watching a TV scene from 'Emergency Room,' and I wondered why they would let me see the dust. The next idea that popped up was that this was a hospital, which is supposed to be clean, and perhaps I ought to let them know about the dust. At that time, I saw no other significance to this apparently random thought.

More people rushed into the room, bringing a cart that contained medical equipment. The body on the bed was violently shaking and people were bent over it, working intently. I began to consider that this patient was really ill and might die. The doctor turned to the cart and everyone else backed away from the bed. With shock, I recognized that the person in the bed was me. Yet there was no fear, sadness, or sense of attachment to the scene below. My mind noted with calmness that I was not looking too good. With that recognition, it felt as if a spiritual vacuum had been turned on and I was sucked back into my body. It happened instantly and forcefully.

I arrived fully consciousness with a vivid memory of my experience. I was so excited, and tried to tell the doctor what had happened. My tongue had some type of depressor on it, preventing me from speaking, and the doctor was not happy with my animation. He kept telling me to be quiet and calm down. All I could think of was what I had just experienced. He finally turned to a nurse and said, "Put her out."

I woke up in a room to the sounds of moaning and crying. Close by, a female voice was plaintively asking the nurse for ice chips. As I opened my eyes, I noticed that people seemed to be surrounded by fluctuating colors in and around their bodies. I thought it was due to the drugs they had given me. My husband was sitting beside my bed. After a few moments, the doctor walked in and told me that I had been given medication to put me into labor. After he left, I became violently sick to my stomach. He then reappeared and told me that the baby had gone into fetal distress and they needed to perform a Cesarean operation. I was so disappointed. I had gone through endless Lamaze classes and had the breathing perfected, but no one had prepared me for this. I felt as if I had failed at the birthing endeavor.

Everything went into hyper-movement as I was prepared for surgery. My husband was asked to leave as I was transported into the surgical room. The surgical nurses were setting up tools for cutting, drawing lines on my body with a felt marker where the scalpel would be applied, and literally pouring iodine over my entire belly. I had an oxygen mask over my face and I remember turning to the anesthesiologist with huge eyes, fearful that I would not be fully unconscious before they began. He reassured me that he understood my fear and that I would be fine.

I made a mental note to remember everything so I could tell my husband later. I also wondered if I would find myself back in the position of floating above, watching the procedure. It gave me a sense of curious anticipation. Instructions were given for me to start counting backwards from ten. I felt an overwhelming calmness and went out.

I woke up on the second evening after surgery. Alone again in a dark room, I began to assess my physical condition. Various wires were running out of my body and somewhere in the vicinity of my thigh, there was a tremendous itch. I felt my stomach and knew that the baby was not there. I tried not to panic, but I needed answers! My vision was blurry and I did not think to find a call button, so I started calling out for help.

A nurse appeared and my first question was about my baby, but she would not tell me if it was alive or well. My husband came in shortly after that and told me he had been with our baby, sharing bits of information on how tiny he was. Being a preemie, my son was in an incubator and I could not see him. The next day they brought me pictures of him. I felt very excluded from my own child's existence. Everyone had interacted with him, he had started his life, and I was not part of it. I even had a thought that possibly the pictures were not real – maybe it was not even my baby! What I was experiencing seemed so different from the happy occasion I had dreamed about. It would be another three days before I was well enough to make the trip to the neonatal unit to see Trenton, my son.

The rest of my hospital stay was fairly uneventful, as far as other dimensional capacity. I was preoccupied with healing and getting to know my tiny son. I tried to tell my husband about my out-of-body experience, but he was not receptive and chalked it all up to drug-induced hallucinations. The only real, physical proof that I could think of was to tell him that I saw dust on the top of the open door. I had been placed back into the same room that I had been in before, and I insisted that he climb up on a chair to check the door. He thought I had lost my senses but finally did as I instructed.

As he swept his hand over the top of the door, a large amount of dirt, rolled up like a dusty snake, fell onto the floor. Instead of seeing it as validating, he reprimanded me and said that now he had to call someone to clean it up. For me, though, it was my first verifying moment. After that, a mental door seemed to open. This small validation was like a whisper of credibility.

For the next forty-five days, I spent my time traveling more than ninety miles from home to hospital to visit my son. I slept on a cot in a storage room next to the neonatal unit, and learned CPR in case he stopped breathing, a common concern with premature babies.

I continued to experience non-stop, vivid and moving colors emanating from living things, plants, animals and humans. This made depth perception very tricky. I was learning to determine where the boundaries for these bodies actually were. Did they begin at the edge of their aura colors or farther in where their physical bodies started? I also had problems with randomly popping out of my body. This left me limited in what I felt safe doing, including being able to drive and take care of my son. After it happened the first time, I was always afraid that it could happen again. I had to make sure that I did not become too tired or stressed, as these seemed to promote this type of phenomenon. Not to minimize these ongoing challenges, it would be more than six months before I experienced another significant event.

CHAPTER TWO

The Fall

"In the end, only three things matter: How much you loved, how gently you lived and how gracefully you let go."
~Master Buddha

My son Trenton arrived home after his first forty-five days in the hospital complete with a heart and respiratory monitor, battery pack, medications to stimulate his heart and respiration, and multiple needs. Unlike most parents, I like to humorously say that my son came home with both instructions and batteries included! Needless to say, this was not a casual situation. The first time he experienced cardiac distress, my husband was present and we were able to bring him out of it by simply lifting him out of his bassinet. There were other times when the alarm on the monitor was loud enough to snap him back to normal function. The first time that I actually had to administer CPR, I was alone with him.

It was early afternoon as I was washing dishes in the kitchen. I heard the alarm go off on Trenton's monitor, and it was not stopping. I went to his room and found my son blue and nonresponsive. Opening the closet door where the CPR instructions were mounted, my mind went blank and I could not read them. Turning back to Trenton, I took a deep breath and focused on what I had been taught, not on how shocking he looked. I did the heart compressions and tiny puffs of air into his nose and mouth, and after three repetitions he revived. I was so scared, and worried that he might have been out for too long. I called 911 and a nurse was sent from the hospital to check on him.

This was the extent of my life during Trenton's first six months at home. I really did not have time to worry about the changes in my psyche from my near-death experience. We could not take Trenton out and I could not leave him with anyone who was not trained to revive him. I lived in a simple, isolated, sleep-deprived world.

Six months later, it was with great anticipation that we finally planned an overnight outing to visit my family. My parents were divorced, but lived fairly close to each other. I was eager to see my Dad and share my son with him. He lived three hours away, and Trenton's battery pack was only good for two hours. I sat in the back seat for the first hour of the journey and monitored his condition, keeping him alert and awake. As he started to get sleepy, I plugged him into the monitor and moved to the front seat next to my husband. I took a much-needed break and observed the landscape as it passed by. I was lulled into a somewhat sleepy, trance-like state by the motion of the car.

I noticed an airplane on the horizon. It was flying low over the hills and I was mesmerized by the lazy, looping path it took in the sky. I thought it was interesting as it was a red bi-plane, the kind that used to give rides at air shows. As my eyes followed it, I was surprised to see a person jump out of the plane. The jumper pulled a parachute and it began to open.

In the next instant, I was inside this person's body. I felt his fear as he realized that his parachute did not open correctly. I now believe that this fear and intense emotion was what sucked me into his mind. It was as if I was a hitchhiker to his final moments. I could feel the wind as it whipped him around and I was aware of his most cherished last thoughts.

He was thinking of his wife and two small boys. I saw their faces, knew their names and how much he loved them. Calmness came over him and his next thought was that they would be taken care of. Then, something struck him from behind. This experience happened in just a split second, but in that time, I viewed his entire lifetime and felt every emotion he had. I did not even know his name; however, I did know his wife's name because he mentally spoke her name as he fell. I was intimately connected to him and was overwhelmed with sadness at his death. Then I found myself back in my own body. I arrived there in hysterics.

I immediately screamed out to my husband, "Pull over! Did you see that? Stop!" I am not sure that he understood why, but he did as I told him to do. I remember thinking that I could run to where the man had landed and help him. Opening the door to the car, I started running out into the open land toward the hill area where I had observed the accident. I was calling frantically to my husband to follow and he kept asking what was wrong. I think he thought that I was sick or needed to find a private place to relieve myself. I remember thinking it was strange that no one else on the road had pulled over. By this time, I was out of breath, which forced me to stop and notice what was going on.

My husband was running towards me, pleading with me to stop. He finally got close enough to grab me. I was trying to tell him the story, gesturing to where the plane was, but as I looked, I realized it was not there. He kept telling me that I had been asleep and not looking out the window. He said I was just dreaming. I felt so foolish and started to cry. Embarrassed, I mumbled something about being so tired and exhausted. Maybe I was just needed some sleep.

We had left the baby in the car by himself and hurried back. He was okay, but I was a wreck. I drank some water, and we sat for a while as I tried to pick the stickers out of my socks from my little sprint through the field, and regain my composure. Relaying in vivid detail, I told my husband how real this experience had been. It was not like any dream I had had before. In fact, it was not dreamlike at all. Instead, it was so specific with facts that I felt as if I knew this man. My husband listened quietly, but his primary concern was that we were off schedule and time had been wasted. This became a recurring theme in our relationship.

When we arrived at my Dad's house, one of the first statements out of my husband's mouth was that we were late because I took off out of the car. My Dad remarked that I must be tired and chalked it up to exhaustion. Later that evening, we went to dinner with friends and, of course, the story was re-told for entertainment.

The next morning, we met my Mom and her friends for breakfast and yes, the story was told again. The story was getting a really good milking! I felt foolish and began to join in on making fun of it all.

On Sunday, we returned home and it was business as usual getting ready for the week to come. Early Monday morning, I received a phone call from my mother. Her friend, Shar, who had been at breakfast with us and had heard the story, was talking excitedly in the background. She had been the only person who had shown interest. Finally, Mom just passed the phone to her friend and let her talk. Her first words were, "You're not going to believe what I'm reading in the newspaper."

She proceeded to read an article that told of a young man who fell to his death from a red bi-plane in Perris Valley, California. He was a stunt man, working for a movie studio. A picture of his wife and two sons accompanied the story. It had happened approximately at the same time we were driving through Acton, not close enough for me to have physically seen the incident. The name of his wife was the same name I heard him think as he fell.

She even validated the sensation I had felt of being hit from behind. There had actually been two men who jumped from the red plane. The second man saw that the first jumper's parachute did not open correctly, and tried to save him. The second jumper grabbed him from behind, but his own parachute became entangled with the defective one. They both fell to their deaths. As I listened to Shar read the article, and the information matched my supposed 'dream,' I had mixed feelings. On one hand I felt relieved, it meant that I was not crazy after all! On the other hand, all the emotions of fear, sadness, and a great sense of loss came flooding back. I was filled with grief.

More calls flooded in from friends and family. The news was out that I was experiencing a possible psychic phenomenon. Everyone had heard about my out-of-body experience while in the hospital, but this definitely began to make my stories have a bit more validity.

My first reaction was fear. Here I was, still struggling with an immense amount of change from the birth of a premature baby, not to mention trying to sort through my out-of-body experience at the hospital. Now, I was faced with another major shift in my reality. I had a huge problem accepting this awareness and attempting to find the good that could result from it. I certainly had not been able to help the men who fell to their deaths!

As I tried to process my feelings, neither my husband nor our parents were much help. As a child, when I told my parents about unusual events, such as seeing people in different colors, they would advise me to keep those thoughts to myself. They treated me like a child who had a very active imagination. After I got married, my parents divorced, and were actively involved in creating their own lives with different partners. My husband was developing his construction business and had no interest in my 'experiences.' He was doing his job as a good provider and expected me to do mine as a good mother.

Today, I have the skills to realize that everything has a purpose and that we are all connected. At the time, however, I needed a concrete reason or purpose to justify this huge distraction that was taking me away from my complicated life. Like most of the people around me, my husband was uncomfortable with a wife who might have psychic qualities that would prevent me from being there for him and our family. In retrospect, I can understand his discomfort, although I did wish I had someone I could talk to. It would not be until my two sons were raised, my parents had passed away, and I was no longer in a committed relationship, that I could truly explore and develop my abilities.

The most important lesson I took away from that first experience in the hospital was that my soul could exist outside of my body. I knew I could also see energies and auras. The parachute jumper experience opened me to a quantum leap in my awareness, which I thought of as being a psychic hitchhiker. I had insight into what others were thinking and feeling. I also was shown that our last thoughts are of our loved ones, and I believe that love is what we take with us when we go. These first experiences initiated a lifelong path to recognizing and assembling my abilities as a multidimensional healer.

CHAPTER THREE

The Surrender

"There may be a time when the only thing you can do is surrender your life to Spirit. Start by accepting who you are and your soul's purpose."
~Master Saint Germain

Trenton's birth set in motion significant occurrences that happened to me and around me, that were in opposition to my beliefs and those of my family and friends. Keep in mind that I was not consciously aware of the big picture, where I was headed or what I was being schooled for. I now know that I have supporters comprised of Spirit Guides, Angels and Ascended Master Teachers, which I refer to as *My Team*, but at the time, I was not aware of them.

My personal clairvoyant experiences had subsided somewhat, but they were not totally gone. I had trouble being in large crowds due to the noise level that emanated from everyone's mind chatter, which made even a trip to the shopping mall eventful. Light and energy still accompanied my vision of people and other things living and inanimate.

Another aspect of my abilities that caused some trouble for me in the beginning was that when information came through me, I was not always aware of what I was saying. The voice speaking through me is not always my voice, and may use words that I would not normally use. Since the voice isn't 'me,' I am detached and do not always remember what I have said, even if it causes major distress for others. Today I understand that I am only the messenger, and I have a bit more control over where and when I receive information. I admit that at times this quality caused me to question myself and shock others.

One day, I was visiting my Dad and his second wife at their house. Her daughter-in-law was four months pregnant and was scheduled for her first ultrasound that day. As I sat at the kitchen table drinking a cup of coffee, she walked past my chair. A heart-wrenching awareness filled my body. When she left the room, I asked my Dad if someone was going with her to the doctor. He said, "I don't think so." The next words that fell out of my mouth were, "Well, someone must go with her, because she is going to find out that her baby is dead." My Dad looked at me like I was a monster and said, "What is wrong with you? Why would you say that?" I felt ashamed. Even *I* could not believe I had said that!

When I am channeling information, I do not always remember what I have said. I forgot about the incident until later that day, when I returned to my Dad's house. He met me at the door and refused me entry. Sadly, what I had predicted had been confirmed by the ultrasound. I had to wait on the front porch while he collected my suitcase and told me to leave. I felt betrayed and that I was being punished for who I was.

On the drive home through the desert, I was quite upset. I believe the stress triggered more psychic activity. A jet from a nearby military base flew low and loud over my car. The aircraft was so close I could see the outline of the pilot in the cockpit. In that moment, I felt that I popped out of my body and was traveling above my car, where the jet had been. At first, I thought, "How cool!" Then, I panicked, and my next thought was, "Whoa, who's driving the car?" I immediately found myself back in the driver's seat and apparently, none the worse. I had somehow maintained my driving while flying above the car.

About fifteen minutes later, I turned off onto a curvy road that ran between two highways. Soon after, a 1970's black Plymouth Barracuda roared up behind me and tailgated me for quite a distance. Just as I was about to pull over and let the vehicle pass, it sped up and went around me on a double yellow line. I saw three young guys in the car as it disappeared around the turn. I knew they were coming up on a hard-to-navigate bend in the road.

At this moment my mind hit the fast forward button and I saw the speeding car lose control, roll in billowing dirt, and land with the tires up. I thought to myself that this was just a mental picture. But, as I reached the location of the crash, I saw that they had indeed wrecked, had crawled out and were sitting next to the upturned car. As I drove by, I was not sure whether I was really seeing this or having another 'episode.' I even drove past them without stopping, while having a serious argument with myself. Finally, I thought, "What if it really did happen?" I felt I could not leave those kids sitting on the roadside.

Turning around, I went back and saw that they were still there. I rolled down my window just enough to yell out and ask if they needed help. Since I still was not sure if this event had really happened, I was quite surprised when they actually answered, said that they were all right, and had help on the way. My parting thought was that they had probably been drinking and did not want police involvement.

Reaching home, I told my husband what I had seen, and he convinced me to report it to the authorities, so I called the Highway Patrol. They took all the information down and several hours later called back to confirm the location. They said they were unable to find the wreck. I assumed that help had arrived and towed the mess away. It was not until a week later that it became clear as to what had really happened.

I got another call from the Highway Patrol and they wanted to check the date that I had reported the accident. They said there was a problem with the date since the accident happened on Tuesday and I had called it in on Monday, twenty-four hours earlier! The clerk was trying to make sense of the report and, at that time, I was confused as well. It was not until I figured out not only what had happened but, also, why it seemed to carry strange feelings with it. I realized I was beginning to recognize the energies of these extrasensory happenings.

The next big episode was one of those rare nights when my husband and I were out on a date. We had met another couple for dinner and drinks. While we were visiting at our table, I became irritated with a man at a nearby table who was smoking up a storm. The restaurant had a no-smoking policy, and I was amazed that no one had noticed that the man was smoking a cigar. It looked to me like he was on fire due to the amount of smoke billowing from his booth.

I finally mentioned to my friends and my husband that I thought we ought to tell someone that this man was smoking. They looked over towards the man, and then just kept on talking! I leaned over and repeated to my husband that we could report him to the bartender. One of my friends turned to me and said, "I know that man. He's my client's husband and he's not smoking right now." Once again, everyone was looking at me as if I was off my rocker. And, of course, it got even worse.

At that instant, I received a download of unasked-for information. I was told that he was a smoker and was dying of lung cancer. Again, this revelation tumbled out of my mouth in a detached way. My husband and friends ignored me and kept eating without a single response. Three months later, that same friend called me in a frenzy. The smoking man's wife had told her that he had been diagnosed with irreversible lung cancer and was dying. This experience made me question, again, what was I supposed to do with these revelations. Would it have made a difference if I had been able to tell him? Would he have listened? Would he have chosen to do anything different?

Today, I am aware that these life situations are opportunities for people to exercise choices. They can use the notice of cancer as a way to heal or they can use it as an exit. I am only the messenger. I now accept that I am the one with the ability to illuminate the options that are available. And, I allow myself to be used as a doorway for the energy that is needed to choose, and pursue the decision that most serves their soul's purpose. This is what I call *Spirit's Grace*.

The next major incident in my early years of psychic development was the one that scared me into deciding that it had to stop. It was shortly after the incident with the smoking man in the restaurant. The first night it happened, I thought that I had just experienced a very vivid nightmare. I dreamed of a little girl, possibly about four years of age. Like the skydiver experience, I felt as if I was inside of her, seeing the world through her eyes.

The dream started with what I thought was me inside a dark, damp shed of some sort. A small strip of light came through the slats in the wall and I could see buckets, plant bulbs and pots. My face was cold and wet from where tears had fallen, and I was sitting up on my legs because the ground was cold and uncomfortable. My underwear was soiled and it bothered me immensely.

Then a bright light came on from outside the shed and I could hear footsteps. A voice that was not mine said, "He's coming, he's coming! Oh no, he's coming." The fear was paralyzing. Along with these words, a flood of images and thoughts arrived. I was inside this little child who remembered her bedroom, complete with a floppy eared bunny, and she wanted to go home. The sound of approaching footsteps brought up visions of a monster-looking man.

The man opened the shed door and through her eyes, he truly did look like a monster. His face was long and distorted and his fingers were also exceptionally long. He put a plate of food in front of her. Her mind reminded her that she was not allowed to take food from strangers. He also put a shoe in front of her and I realized that a shoe was missing from one of her feet. The end of the first night's dream was the sound of the door being padlocked and the lights being turned off. I was only aware of the darkness.

The first vision was distressing enough that I woke my husband up. I did not want to lose the thought of this child and I felt I had to share it with someone. Somehow it seemed important. My husband was tired and was not very interested in my story. I knew this was different than a normal dream and I kept saying that it was like the others, meaning the other psychic experiences.

Three more nights ensued, and the visions came each evening. After my husband's reaction the first time, I did not wake him again. The little girl was becoming more irrational and hysterical. The monster man would attempt to touch her and all of a sudden my mind would go to what I called a white screen. It was as if her mind had just blanked out or possibly shut down. After each time, I would find myself back in my body, in my bed, full of a child's emotions. Not only was I immersed in her hopeless mindset, I also knew I was powerless to do anything about it.

I could not make sense of these psychic events. I did not know who or where the little girl was, had no idea what she looked like, which is one of the disadvantages of seeing everything through the other person's eyes. I had no details of her abductor's face, as she always saw him as a distorted monster.

Just when I thought that I could not take anymore, the fifth night the dream did not come. I woke and lay in the darkness of my bedroom, experiencing more dread and anguish than when I had been part of her horror. I instinctively knew that her absence from my mind was not a good sign. I wondered if it meant that she was no longer alive. My husband was relieved that I was not bothered anymore with these 'dreams,' since he failed to acknowledge that they were anything more significant.

After nights of experiencing this poor child's misery, I knew I could not take any more visions. If I could have seen a positive benefit from them, either for me or for the person whose life I was sharing, then I might have allowed them to continue. But, as it was, this 'ability' appeared to be unending and without purpose. After I overheard family members discussing getting a full-time nanny and putting me in an institution, I desperately began searching for a solution.

My maternal grandmother had a family reputation for being able to foretell the future, which included prophesying what I considered to be negative times such as accidents, sickness, and relationship difficulties. She was convinced that her ability was her matriarchal gift from a religious-based God. She was not exactly who I would have considered my first go-to contact for help. The common thought in our family was that God spoke to Grandma. This was a fairly intimidating idea as a child, to think your grandmother has a direct line to God! So, my reluctance to share my experiences with her was that I did not want to have Grandma's judgment or God's wrath heaped on top of my already overloaded emotional situation.

With no other options, I finally did approach Grandma. I knew that my mother had kept her informed about the challenging times I was in. To my surprise, when I began to share incidents with her, she appeared to understand and was not shocked at all. She asked me two specific questions. First, were these situations interfering with my marriage? And second, were they getting in the way of my being a mother and raising my child? My answer affirmed both. Her response and solution was to pray, ask to have 'it' removed, and it would happen. She explained that she had asked God to limit her clairsentiency to just family issues, and He had done so.

So, I prayed to surrender my abilities if there was no possible way to help someone. With relief and a bit of surprise, my prayers were answered. Things became very quiet in my life, allowing me to catch up, regroup and raise my son through the challenges of his premature birth to a safe age. As life found me waving goodbye to him on his first day of kindergarten, I learned that I was pregnant again.

CHAPTER FOUR

The Gleaning

"Remember who you are. Gather your tools, retrieve your ancient abilities and perfect your soul skills."
~Master Kathumi

Gleaning: *1. To gather or collect something in a gradual way. 2. To search something carefully. 3. To gather materials that have been left behind.*

Due to the difficulty of my first delivery, I had been told that I would never be able to get pregnant again, and if I did, would never be able to carry to full term. Not surprisingly, I was fearful of what this second pregnancy would bring. I was also having marital difficulties, and I had decided my husband and I were headed towards separation. I was devastated by the realization that for over four years I believed I was not capable of conceiving. Now that I was making plans to live on my own, a miracle baby arrives!

After some soul searching, I came to grips with it all and figured that I had to see the pregnancy through to whatever end would come. I wanted to bring this child into the living world. My husband was happy, my first-born was upset that he was not going to be the center of mom and dad's attention, and I was back to struggling with everyone's needs. I felt my newfound self-awareness slipping away. I just kept thinking, "Here we go again!"

I started my second pregnancy with much clearer expectations for what I was dealing with. We found a new doctor who had the latest technology in his clinic, and I had no illusions about the possibility of a natural, joyful and much anticipated birthing that so many of my friends had experienced. There were doubts that hovered in my mind from my first encounter with motherhood. In some ways, though, it was beneficial to have had that experience first. As this pregnancy progressed, I could not help but notice that it was much easier.

When my precious red-haired son arrived, I was able to be conscious and greet him at delivery. My second son, Weston, was premature by a month, so I was not able to hold him as he was placed in a temporary incubator. However, the two weeks that he spent in the hospital prior to coming home felt like nothing compared to the almost two months required for my first son. By my definition, it felt like a 'normal' delivery.

By the time my son Weston was born, I had developed some experience with my abilities as a clairvoyant and psychic hitchhiker. It seemed as though my experiences were following the path of my grandmother's, tied to just the lives of my children and close family. There was less fear, more manageability, and I developed a comfort zone I could live with.

I began to go back and review my life for other experiences I may have had that would give me some insight into my current life situation. It was as if I was gathering bits of my soul that had been left behind. I use the word *gleaning* to describe the method of going back and retrieving early fragments and life experiences, understanding their significance, and integrating them to create wholeness.

The earliest memory I have that relates to the presence of my Spirit Guides was when my grandmother spoke of my imaginary friend I had as a little girl. She called him my Guardian Angel. I now feel confident that my Guardian Angel was in fact one of my Spirit Guides.

As a child, I could see people in colors. Up to age four, I would refer to angry people as 'red,' and people I was attracted to as 'shiny.' After starting school, I came home one day, embarrassed, and told my parents that I had been teased because of my color talk. They listened and suggested that I not bring it up any more. I did not recall this childhood memory until I saw colors around people again, eighteen years later, after my near death occurrence. So, note to parents: If your child describes unusual experiences, be supportive. It could possibly make their life easier rather than more difficult. I know it would have been so in my case.

In my opinion, early childhood experiences are so very significant in establishing and keeping a connection to a soul level existence. At the beginning stage of life, children are clear of physical attachments. And, they have not been told that the thoughts, feelings and things they are seeing are not real. They have a foot in both existences, and if these experiences are accepted by others, that ability can be retained and expanded. As I give readings to clients today, they often share with me that they had early childhood memories or experiences they could not explain. Too often, we are forced by society, our peer groups and even those who love us, to forget who we are.

I can see how my exposure to multiple religions, schools with religious aspects, and even my association with the Job's Daughters and the Masonic Youth organizations helped broaden and shape my path. My paternal grandmother was a devout Jehovah's

Witness, and my maternal grandmother had an interest in Seventh Day Adventism. My husband and I attended the Methodist church, where his father often gave sermons. There was a time when I thought about being Jewish and looked into the Kabbalah and its teachings. I studied Buddhism and delved deeply into ritualistic principles of many religious philosophies. If nothing else, these forays into religious doctrines gave me a clear understanding of what was *not* right for me. I believe that exploring different cultures and religions can help shed light on our own belief systems.

One day my grandmother called me and told me that she was dying. She asked me to be her caregiver and specifically wanted me to be with her when she died. While I was caring for her she lapsed into a coma. I was reading to her from her Bible when her breathing progressed to the well-known death rasp, and I knew she was close to passing. As I read, I thought someone had walked into the room, and I glanced up. To my surprise, I saw my grandmother standing by my side with her hands on her hips. For just one instant I wondered how she had gotten out of the bed! She was looking at her body in the bed and shaking her head back and forth. Then, it dawned on me that she was preparing to go. When she actually passed, I saw her spirit leave her body. It manifested as a bolt of light that shot up and disappeared. This was a powerful experience and the first time I had assisted someone making the transition.

Looking back with my present day knowledge of myself and the journey that followed, I have come to realize that she was, in many ways, a mirror of me. We look alike, and we are both very strong women. I am named after her, and, we have both experienced the capability to sense and/or feel beyond the physical realm.

During my second pregnancy, I was about six months along when I experienced another psychic hitchhike event. My husband was making sausage for dinner and the smell was making me nauseous. I went into the bedroom and laid down to rest. I felt as if I was dreaming when I found myself inside a man's perception. Almost immediately, I recognized that it was my Dad. He was talking to a short, blond woman who was folding towels on a pool table. She had a red, heart-shaped ring on her finger. I could see every detail in the room.

They were discussing what to bring on a proposed camping trip and I could hear wind chimes and a bird squawking in the background. Through my father's eyes I saw a house with many plants. Also, I noticed his attention seemed to be focused on her braless chest, covered only by a tank top. Needless to say, this was not a comfortable scene for me. After being divorced for ten years, my mother and father had just started dating again. Since my insight did not come with a timeline, I had no idea whether this conversation had occurred in the past or was taking place in present time. I woke up from this flash of information and jotted down what I could remember in my dream journal. I even made little drawings of the lady's ring. I knew I would be seeing my Dad within the next few days, as he had planned a visit to see me. I intended to ask him about what I had seen.

As he sat at my dinner table during this much-anticipated visit, I remembered my dream journal and excitedly grabbed it to show my Dad. I actually handed the notes to him and he started reading them. As he read, I watched my father's face morph into a very agitated, angry state. He actually accused me of driving, at six months pregnant, the three hours to this lady's house just to spy on him! His anger was due in part to my revealing that he was having a relationship with the lady with the heart-shaped ring at the same time he was dating my mother.

My mind was multi-tasking. At the very same moment that I registered my father's angry reaction, I also realized that the information I had received had been accurate. This was exciting and validating. It was not until my father stormed out of the house that I knew I had hit a nerve. Little did I know at the time that this incident would place such a distance between us, that my father would no longer share details of his personal life with me.

This experience reminded me of all the times that people in my life were unwilling to accept my abilities. In the gleaning process, I strove to recover lost pieces of myself and gathered valuable information. I made a decision to treat my children differently when or if their supernatural gifts started to appear.

By this time, Trenton had developed a very special level of communication with me. He seemed to be tuned into the thoughts that ran through my head. Eventually, I came to realize that he saw images from my mind, and that was how he understood, not by words. He often let me know that he knew what I was thinking.

When Trenton was in kindergarten, he told me about a dream he'd had, and showed me a map that he was drawing. He explained that this was the neighborhood where 'Jarred' lived. His description included Jarred's best friend's house, school, and most uniquely, the 7-Eleven where Jarred bought really big, plastic cups of soda. Now, we lived in a town where we had just one Circle K store. We did not allow him to watch TV and he was limited to Sesame Street and Disney videos. There was no way he would have had knowledge of a 7-Eleven store. In fact, when he first told me, he called it the "seven-one-one store." When I questioned him, he offered stories of how Jarred had told him, "…me and my friends would hang out in the parking lot, drink big sodas, and we could get refills cheap." Trenton also said that Jarred would take him on flights over his town. When he talked about it, it was always from the perspective of a teenage boy. I began to wonder if there was more to Jarred than the limited imagination of my four-year-old son. I found out later, that in fact, there actually was.

I now know that these gleaning experiences helped me to make a pivotal decision to accept my gifts. A new awareness was rising in me and I began to believe that I could exist in two worlds, raising my boys and being clairsentient. Along with these thoughts I also had the revelation that there were people in my life who would not be helpful to me on my journey. With sadness, I realized that I had to distance myself from many of my closest family and friends. This awareness manifested with a zero tolerance for anyone, or any situation that did not support my new direction. Today, when I work with students, I give them a mantra to recite which was an important element in my evolving viewpoint at that time. I am not sure of its original origins. It is: *"I ask that I attract all people, places and things that are Divine and right in my life. And, all other people, places and things depart from me now."* I repeated this phrase nine times a day for nine months.

As a result of this gleaning process, friends, family and acquaintances that were not accepting of who I was and what I needed to do to be my authentic self began to fall away. Some were important figures in both my life and the lives of my sons. This included my husband of eleven and a half years.

When Todd and I married, I was polite and well mannered. It didn't hurt that I had a few beauty pageant wins under my belt. We met through our mutual participation in the Masonic youth organizations. Both our families were entrenched in these principles and beliefs, and his world was quite defined. As Valley League DeMolay Sweetheart, I epitomized his choice for a wife. He was a simple man and he expected a simple life. He had not bargained on or signed up for the psychic roller coaster ride I woke up on. He made it clear that he was not going to get on the ride, and I do not blame him. I definitely feel blessed that I have two wonderful sons from our time together and all is as it is supposed to be.

I gradually came to accept that I could not be authentic without ensuring that the spiritual path would be the most important factor of my life. Even though my path was revealed to me at the time of my near-death experience with the birth of my first son, it took another nine years until I built up enough courage to stand in my power, leave the desert, and place my healing work at the center of my existence. In those years, I found out what it was I wanted to do, and who I had to be to achieve it. I began to believe in a life that was guided by Spirit. Most importantly, through the gleaning, I realized that I was the person responsible for making it happen.

CHAPTER FIVE

Healing

"Healing is a process that begins with forgiving yourself and remembering your original state of being one with The Divine."
~Master Yeshua Jesus The Christ

Healing is always an inside job, no matter who you are, how much money you have, your position in society, your age, sex, or how well you dress. Many a rich, brilliant and powerful person has tried to bypass the process of healing. Why? Well, speaking from my own experience and from what I have observed, for many of us, it is not easy and it carries pain with it.

Our world is full of people on anti-depressants and sleeping pills as a result of being unwilling to stop, reflect on painful topics and *feel*. I never recommend that someone stop their medications, and know there are crisis moments when treating the physical body with drugs can be life-sustaining. There are also a small percentage of people with mental illnesses who require medication for survival. However, the majority of people on medication are not incurable. We want to feel, it is just that we only want to feel what we consider to be the good, fun feelings.

We prefer to skip over the part of experiencing the so-called bad feelings and get to the 'good.' The proverbial drink or pill, material things and other people are some of the methods we use to avoid the pain of healing.

Sometimes, when we experience painful or bad feelings, we can get stuck in them, as if we are locked into a cycle we cannot break. These repetitive responses might have given temporary relief in our past, but eventually they are no longer useful or give the aid they used to. In our efforts to avoid pain, we keep trying to make the old patterns work. Lacking the tools to break through our old belief systems, we spin in repetitive holding patterns, until the desire to heal becomes strong enough to overcome our resistance.

To fulfill my destiny as a healer for others, I had to heal myself first. I had been living under the influence of my parents, husband, and community. After my divorce, I found myself truly on my own for the first time. On the outside, I appeared to be a capable young woman of twenty-nine, but on the inside I needed to discover who I really was. I spent the next five years doing what I now think of as making up for lost time. My sons spent every other weekend with their father, so my life became multifaceted. One weekend I was baking cookies, mowing the lawn, and being a good mommy. The other weekend, I explored a myriad of careers and opportunities in my newfound free and single life. Much like a teenager, I tried on different lifestyles and jobs to learn what I liked and what did not work for me.

I became interested in aromatherapy and began making scented candles and soap. I had a workplace in the garage with a large stainless steel pot where I would melt tallow for soap and beeswax for candles. I added essential oils, then poured the soap and wax into molds to cool and cure. To this day I love good, hand made soap, beeswax candles, and use essential oils in my daily life.

While I was working on my candle and soap projects, the neighbor kids would come over to play with my boys. When they saw me stirring my big steaming pot and pouring scented oils into it, they started a rumor that I was a witch. Just to add to the fun, at Halloween I would dress up like a witch and their imaginations would run wild.

My first job after my divorce was as a bartender at a hotel bar and restaurant in the small desert town where I lived. I also worked as an optical technician, a secretary at a real estate office, and even drove a water truck for a pumice mine on the midnight shift. I tried my talents at teaching swing and country dancing, appeared in a of couple music videos, managed some bands, and totally immersed myself in the single life. I enrolled in criminal justice and abnormal psychology classes at the local city college, thinking that my abilities might serve others as a crime scene investigator. Looking back, I can see that I was trying to stay so busy that those spiritual experiences would stay in the background. I tried to dance my way through living, hoping my unusual past would not catch up with me.

One of my regular customers at the bar was Bobby Brand, a civil engineer, who was a contractor for the county. One day he said he needed an assistant to help hold his gear, and I jumped at the chance to learn something new. I would hold the elevation stick while he mapped the contours of the land. I set up the equipment, attached the theodolite (which he referred to as 'the instrument') on its tripod, then used the plumb bob to vertically align it to the survey mark on the ground. This apparatus was used to triangulate measures of distance and elevation.

One day Bobby drove out further into the desert than ever before. I had no idea where we were. As he stopped the truck he reached behind the front seat and pulled out a metal coat hanger. He unscrewed the neck of the hanger and bent it into two separate 'L' shapes. He loosely held the short end of the L shaped wire in his hands. With the longer end of the L pointed out in front of him, he walked back and forth, and around in circles. The metal pieces moved to and fro like little antennae. I watched him do this for some time while giggling and heckling him. I thought he was pulling a prank on me. When I asked him what he was doing, he grinned and told me to get the shovel and duct tape out of the truck. He stuck the shovel into the ground and told me, "Dig here!"

Now, up until this point I thought this was all fun and games. As I began digging, I realized just how far out in the middle of nowhere we were. I reprimanded myself about how sometimes my instincts were not as good as I thought they were. What was the duct tape for...? I wondered how well I knew Bobby, and if anyone knew where I was. Most of this I muttered aloud while he kept quiet and smirked at me in a suspicious manner. Suddenly, my shovel struck something. I wiped the dirt away and found the metal marker for an old gold mine. I looked up at Bobby and he grinned back at me. He had used his dowsing abilities to locate a lost mine, and had let me uncover it.

I was so fascinated by Bobby's ability to sense and read the energy of the earth that I asked him to teach me how to do it. This was the beginning of my education in dowsing. Bobby taught me how to use the electromagnetic power grid of the earth to find water and metals. It was through dowsing that I developed my ability to feel and see the energy that runs in the earth. It expanded to my being able to detect ley lines on the earth's planetary grids, and to help students detect the flow of their body's energy by using pendulums. Oh, and the duct tape, Bobby just threw that in for fun!

When I was a bartender, people would show up to talk to me about their love life. I told them they needed to buy a drink to keep my boss happy. I discovered I could see energetic attractions and compatibilities between people, which made me something of a matchmaker. In fact several couples that I introduced ended up getting married. After a while I developed a bit of a reputation as a person of interest in town.

Our town was only a few hours north of Los Angeles and was an inexpensive location for filming. Film production crews would come to town periodically, and would eat and drink in the restaurant and bar where I worked. During the shooting of a film, tragedy struck when a member of the film crew was electrocuted. The crew had spent so much time together that they had become like a family. The incident devastated them. Shooting stopped, and the actors and most of the crew left. A small group of men stayed in town to take care of the equipment and preserve the location. While consoling these men who had suffered an emotional loss, I discovered that I could receive information by touching them. These people were essentially strangers to me, yet, when I touched them, I was able to sense what they felt. It was the first time I considered the possibility that I could use my abilities to help others.

The next time a movie crew came to town, I was asked to help the company's massage therapist. The film had a crew of people dressed as apes, with heavy headpieces. The massage therapist's job was to keep them comfortable during the long waiting periods between takes. Naomi, the massage therapist, was a striking woman and a Native American Shaman. I watched her give a massage where she used shamanic healing tools. I saw the energy being exchanged in waves of light between her and her client.

One day Naomi called me on the phone at the bar. She was talking very softly, almost whispering. She asked me to come to a room in the hotel after my shift. She told me to bring six brandy snifters and a bottle of 151-proof rum to the room. She said she would leave the door ajar and for me to come in without knocking. I thought I was being invited to a private party. When I entered the room, it was dark, and Native American drumming music was playing. I looked at the massage table in the center of the room and saw a gigantic, bare, African American man lying face down. He was so large that he completely covered the table and appeared to be floating in midair. I watched as Naomi poured a small amount of rum in each snifter and light it with a match. She quickly placed the inverted glass on the man's back, which was covered with oil. His skin was sucked up into the glass. It was the first time I had witnessed the technique called 'cupping,' which is used to draw out impurities. That was my introduction to massage therapy. I realized that massage could provide me with an opportunity to combine my healing goals and abilities. I could finally see a way to use by abilities to sense what people were feeling, see the energy patterns in their bodies and use touch for healing.

I found a massage school and drove the four-hour round trip three days a week. To complete the internship, I had to perform one hundred massages on clients who came to the school for discounted services. As I focused on their maladies, I found I could discover the location of their pain rather easily. I also discovered that as my clients left the sessions feeling much relieved, I seemed to absorb their physical problem. If their complaint had been a sore shoulder, my shoulder would be sore and painful after they left. I had internalized their pain and somehow transferred it to myself.

At the end of one particularly long and busy day, my instructor noticed that I was dragging a sore and stiff body around — my own! She questioned my processes in the massage treatment and began to comprehend that I was empathically picking up on my clients' pain. I shared with her that not only could I feel heat and/or electrical impulses from their injured areas, but I also saw a red glow or even shadows. She informed me that I was not going to be able to continue with this profession unless I learned how to release the negative energy I took on.

She taught me how to envision bringing in white light through the top of my head, letting it flow over my body, and watch it clear the pain. I saw it as a waterfall of liquid white light, cleansing and removing trapped energy. She also told me how to ground this energy, sending it down into the earth through my grounding cord. This is an energetic connection to the earth that all of us have.

I started using this method for cleansing myself after every massage. Then I had an idea: Why not just let that waterfall flow all the time? Why wait until I was sore or already encumbered? I experimented with this concept, even trying to send the waterfall through a client. I figured that if it worked for me, why couldn't it work for her, too? The results were amazing! She commented that she felt a tingling over her body and as if she was floating just on the edge of consciousness. After we finished, she felt much more rejuvenated than previous times. Client after client began to give me consistent feedback. Many asked me what I was doing different. Looking back, I know that this was the beginning of my understanding of the relationship between energy movement and healing.

While I was in massage school I went through several weeks of visitations from my grandmother, who had been dead for more than six years at the time. These visits were very early in the morning, just before dawn, and at first I thought they were dreams. She would sit on the edge of my bed and lightly stroke the inside of my forearm while she spoke lovingly to me. As she left, I would slowly come out of my trance-like state and could smell the lingering scent of lilacs. I would catch the last few words or possibly a sentence before she left that went something like this, "Now, don't forget what I said," or "Don't miss this window in time." The messages felt more and more urgent as the visits went on. I believed that she was telling me something really important and that I wasn't remembering or understanding exactly what she was trying to convey to me.

I spoke about these visits with my cousin Lindy, who is like a sister to me. Lindy had heard of a psychic who supposedly connected people with their loved ones on the other side. She made an appointment for us to see her. I was surprised, because Lindy was uncomfortable with the idea of psychics and felt that they were taboo. That she would stretch so far out of her comfort zone was a genuine sign of her love.

When we arrived at Susan's charming home located in a regular neighborhood, it all seemed so normal and pleasant. It was not at all what I expected. I thought that people who had this capability lived in tents, wore black, spoke with accents and gazed into crystal balls. Susan was a spry, elderly woman who looked like everyone's grandma. She offered us tea as we sat on the sofa in her living room. Before I said anything to her about why I was there, she said that my grandmother was anxious to speak to me.

Susan relayed a message from my grandmother that I was with the *wrong* Michael and that I had a short time to get ready to make my move to the coast. This guidance felt right and made sense with what I was going through in my life at that time. Susan also gave me an interesting reading that sounded amazing, but I felt like it was for someone else. She told me that people would be paying me for my advice and that I would be flying locally and internationally to speak about my work.

It wasn't until a couple years later that the things Susan told me in my reading began to manifest. With anticipation, I tried to find her for another reading, but I was unable to. I finally gave up, believing she had made her transition to the other side. It took several more years to realize she had given me an amazingly accurate reading. Susan also showed me that psychics can live normal lives without the stereotypical fortune teller, new age or hermit stereotype that some people associate with these gifts. I didn't know it then, but as time went on I came to understand that Susan was a meaningful role model or 'way seer' for me. She helped show me the way on my path.

Up until this point my boys and I had lived near their father in a strict military settlement that housed a weapons facility. Needless to say, massage was not considered a spiritualistic healing tool and had other connotations. After the terrorist attack of September 11, 2001, the town became a frenzy of high alert. They actually drove tanks down the streets, and the distress in the community was evident. I made a quick decision to move to an area that would not only support my occupation but my emotional health as well. I found my new home in a town located on the coast of California.

I subleased a small office next to a hair salon, and my first business venture as an intuitive massage therapist was born. However, I still felt that I had not found the right location. I wanted to be in a community that was motivated towards health, natural remedies and was more open to energetic healing. I developed a relationship with a man named Michael who lived in just that type of area. Per my grandmother's guidance, I realized he was the right Michael, and I would not have found him if I had stayed in the desert. A position with a massage center opened up and I took it. I moved there, and gradually developed a client list.

As a result of my relationship with Michael, I went to Okinawa, Japan several times and learned a new aspect of meditation. Japanese philosophies believe that simple every day occurrences are opportunities to reach a meditative state. Pouring tea, working in gardens and serving food were slowed down with intention and purpose, creating a moving meditation that became a true way of life. I incorporated these philosophies into my own life.

Michael and I owned a boat we kept in a slip in a harbor that became a haven from stress and human contact. More importantly, being connected to water the boat gave me an energy conduit that produced wonderful dreams and healing sleep time. I had the sensation of being in a womb-like environment that provided certain frequencies for recharging my energy and finding solutions to the changing life I was living.

I pursued this life for several years while my healing abilities continued to grow. It was here that I had an encounter with a regular massage client who complained of not feeling well. In the middle of her massage, I observed the now familiar red glow around her mid-section. However, this time the sighting came with a comforting voice in my head, telling me that it was her gall bladder. I recognized that it was the same voice that had given me other predictions in the past. As before, I blurted out the knowledge to the client that she needed to have her doctor check out her gall bladder. She seemed unimpressed with my diagnosis. After I pressed the point a bit more, she agreed to get it checked out.

Prior to this encounter she had been coming to me once a week, for months. Her visits suddenly stopped, and I surmised that I had crossed a line with her, or that she had become uncomfortable with me. Two months later, she called to make an appointment and said she needed to see me. She came with a gift and a thank you card. Apparently, her gall bladder had developed a tumor and my warning had prompted her to see her doctor. It had subsequently been removed and she was feeling much better. I was scared and excited at the same time. I felt that my abilities jumped to the next level!

Even though I had several more successful medical intuition incidents, I still doubted myself. What if I heard the voice wrong? What if I am just plain nuts? It did not happen all the time and I did not seem to have control over it. Telling someone they may have a physical malady elevated the level of responsibility beyond giving relationship advice, massage and moving energy. I decided to explore this possibility further, and knew I would need a private setting to achieve my goals. I created Amethyst Intuitive Massage in a small and separate section of my home.

My client list increased as people started referring others. I had requests for not only intuitive massage but energy work as well. The strangely familiar voice in my head, which had identified my client's gall bladder problem, advanced and evolved to become a purple-hued man dressed like pirate who was visible only to me. Our relationship progressed to where he actually placed his hands on mine as I placed my hands on the client. Honestly, it was more as if he put his hands *into* mine. I could see his energy run through my client's body and spread like a purple flame. When this happened, the client, with eyes closed, would comment that they were actually seeing purple flickers.

He began to communicate with me during my morning meditations and I kept asking who he was. He would tell me his name and for some reason, I simply could not understand what he told me. Finally, he said to just call him Mr. R. It was not until three years later that I found out who he was.

During the time I was working with Mr. R., we developed an intimate relationship, and he was instrumental in guiding me to find the best location for my healing center. This might be difficult for some to comprehend, but he became my mentor, friend and constant companion. He was, quite literally, my savior during what I called my thirteen months of shadows.

This period began with my mother's death from a rare illness. My oldest son, Trenton, was only nineteen when he informed me that I was going to be a grandmother, and my youngest, Weston moved to his father's house four hours away. My relationship of five years with Michael ended, and I had to find new locations for my home and office. The shadow times culminated with the unexpected death of my father.

In the night, when my emotions were so strong, Mr. R. would

place his healing energy around me, and was my protector. When I had thoughts of sadness, he would console me. He was as real to me as any living being I have ever known, and still is. He showed me how to take strength from the challenging events of these months and to channel it into re-inventing myself into who I was meant to be.

My life became my awakening, and I dove into my work. Finally, I was able to be my authentic self without fear of any repercussions. My parents, whose opinions mattered to me, were deceased and there was no possibility of hurting them. My children were on their own or with their father. I was finally capable of putting the energy and effort I required into the final touches of my transformation. With this new-found liberation I could now dedicate my life to what I truly believed.

Today, I consider myself to be a multidimensional healer, teacher and channel for Spirit. My quantum hitchhiking experience facilitated my ability to perform long distance healing work. It enables me to connect with others in the etheric realm and to heal people all over the world.

PART TWO

The Transformation

Transformation: *1. A change in character or condition. 2. Transmute into a higher element or thing. 3. Fitting something for a new or different use.*

CHAPTER SIX

Soul Examination

"Within every human is the power to express in every moment that which is the Master – intensified, individual focus of self or conscious intelligence."
~Master El Morya

Soul examination is a gift to us from Spirit. Certain things can only be learned by being in the physical body. We come here as a soul in a body to learn these things. Spirit graces us with the opportunity to choose the path that aligns us with our soul's purpose. Soul examination is the first step to soul healing.

Webster's definition of **Soul** is: *The immaterial essence, animating principle or actuating cause of an individual life.* Apparently, the definition of Soul is a challenge even for the professionals! Yet, few would declare that the soul does not exist. So, let us start with…what *is* a soul? I would like to share with you my perspective on the energies of the physical body, Soul, Source, Spirit and consciousness, and how they relate to one another.

All energy emanates from the **Source**. It is a non-judgmental loving energy that is in all things, is all encompassing and omnipotent. Source has been given many names. For example: God, Divine Masculine or Feminine, Universe, Higher Power, Father Sky, etc. Other cultures have their own names for it as well. I usually refer to it as simply, Source. Source exists not only on the physical level, but it also powers all etheric and dimensional worlds.

Our soul is an individual spark of this Divine Source, and it links us to this vast expanse in many ways. Truthfully, through the soul, we are connected to *All That Is*. I realize that this concept may make the dictionary's classification somewhat basic and lacking in detail. However, understanding the magnitude of our soul's capacity is critical to believing in the power to heal.

Imagine you are standing at the edge of a pool of water that is fed by a tall, cascading waterfall. The waterfall is The Source and the pool is The Soul. As a physical being, we need water to sustain us. By dipping our hand into the pool, we ingest the small amount needed to survive. The water in our hand is our consciousness in this physical reality. It is our connection to our soul and, more importantly, to Source. Even though it is a small amount, it still contains all the elements of the waterfall.

Our souls are not confined to our bodies. At a soul level, we share our pools with others. Like the drop that contains all the elements of the waterfall, we as humans have all the atoms, particles and molecules that created the universe, making us one with Source, or *All That Is!*

We have been given an amazing opportunity to experience life on the physical level. Many other beings in other realms and dimensions do not have the chance to be born into a body or to experience life in quite the same way we do. We come into our bodies with a mission, like scientists, to explore the universe. Compared to bodiless entities, living in a body is like attempting to move and function in a deep sea diving suit, or what I like to call a bio-suit. Our soul is connected to the bio-suit through our consciousness. This bio-suit slows down the soul's absorption rate, leading to loss of focus and distraction. Meditation and lucid dreamtime offer opportunities to surface, get clear input and breathe. It gives us the ability to handle the slow, plodding, physical environment we are in.

In our bio-suits we feel sensations intensely with our skin, central nervous systems and brains. We have hormones that trigger powerful emotions and sensations. Smell, taste, and touch are more potent, sweeter, softer, brighter and more passionate. Pain, loss and emptiness are also experienced acutely on the physical plane.

Think of this example: When the astronauts explore space, they are wired with sensors that send data back to the home base on Earth. The scientists at ground control are recording every body function, movement and emotion of the astronaut. The individual soul is wired to all other souls through the Source in somewhat the same way. All of our individual and collective experiences are recorded, stored, and transmitted to other souls in other realms. These souls then get a taste of the familiarity of the physical plane. It is similar to the cybernetic re-creation of reality we call virtual reality.

Now that we have a working concept of a soul, the next question might be, "What is the purpose of a soul?" With each new incarnation we forget our relationship to Source. As humans we have an exclusive experience that includes feelings of loss and separateness. I believe the purpose of the soul is driven by our passion to reclaim our connection to Source in a deeper and more profound way. This requires us to evolve and grow through our life experiences. Life's dichotomies occur so that we will become motivated to resolve the opposites that create conflict in our lives, and find our way back to Source.

Source also experiences itself through *us*. Source has a desire to experience itself in another form, a form that can sensually perceive existence in an inclusive way. As humans, we also have a desire to experience a part of ourselves in someone else. This is why many decide to have children, choose to teach or see themselves reflected through a creative outlet. Devoting one's self to service to others is a way of enriching our relationship with Source.

Source energy graduates to Spirit, then to our individual souls and becomes our consciousness. **Spirit** is the energy that connects us all; it is Source in motion and includes not only individual souls but also is the connection between our souls. When it flows through our bodies, it is our individual spark that interprets and perceives emotions, sensations, awareness of ourselves, and the world around us.

When I began my own soul examination as a healer, I realized that my ability to do my work must be a priority. I have learned that my life energy needs to be functioning at 100% before I can heal at the highest level. For me, this requires a balance achieved by living according to specific rules. This includes being able to disconnect from TV, computer and current events. I meditate, clear my energy fields and connect to my Spirit Guides and Angels, which I refer to as *My Team,* daily. I also receive personal healing at this time, working on any issues that I might have which would restrict my flow of energy. Personal relationships have to be placed in a secondary spot and are attended to after these daily maintenance requirements. These practices are fundamental to my success and the success of anyone in the healing field. I have observed, as well as experienced, that this can be a difficult lesson, but it is essential for those in the healing community to develop their skills.

So, we have this wonderful bio-suit that allows us to connect to other people, places and things on so many levels, but we can only comprehend it with our human abilities, including our capacity to recognize truth. How then, do we take these ordinary abilities and travel to the planes of other dimensions? This is where consciousness comes into the mix. It is our vehicle that will take us to unknown heights.

Consciousness is Soul in physical form, the part of us that is aware of the larger picture behind the earthly drama. It is always present, yet our minds and bodies are not always aware of it. In spiritual terms, consciousness is self-aware atoms of energy emanating from Source. It has been given many names throughout time, and is often interchanged in speaking of the soul, but for the sake of clarity we will stick to calling it our consciousness.

Some people believe that they have opened temporary doorways to higher consciousness using sex, drugs and rock and roll. I can't see any harm in safe sex or rock and roll, but I advise everyone to be careful with the use of drugs, either natural or prescribed. They may be letting your body believe that it does not need to produce hormones or chemicals naturally, and could cause dependency that can interfere with normal body function.

Alcohol has a different effect on the physical body. The feeling of being 'buzzed' is actually caused by dehydration of the brain. As we all know, water is a conduit of energy. So drinking alcohol actually has the opposite effect. In fact, it's one of the most common ways people use to 'check out' of states of higher consciousness.

Your illuminated self is needed on this amazing and intricate planet as we all strive to connect to Source. As each person upgrades their energy circuits, they raise the energy of those around them as well. This is how we raise the consciousness of the entire planet.

When we are not aware of our connection to our soul, then we cannot live consciously or in truth. Any incident or emotion we put our attention on is what we unintentionally invite into our lives. When we put our focus on our fears, they will manifest.

When we put our focus on things that bring us joy, they will also multiply. In each moment we become that which we are focused on. Consciousness, our connection to our soul, is the passion hidden behind the boring routine, the still voice of peace suppressed by the rage and the will to survive beyond the despair. Our consciousness shows itself through our creativity, our inner and outer glow, the way our energy shines through our bodies, and when we have a knowing about something or someone. It reveals itself in our "A-ha" moments.

Our thirst for awareness and connection to Source determines how much we dip into the pool of consciousness. Once we get a taste of how delicious and fulfilling it is, our goal becomes trying to take in as much consciousness as possible. We start to see how we can manifest the soul's desires. This is the point where we start to work towards our higher purposes through spiritual practice. We begin to connect the mind, body, emotions and consciousness, so that healing can begin.

Once our thirst for consciousness has been ignited, it begins to shine the light on our soul. Through soul examination, we begin the process of reclaiming bits of our soul we have left behind. Reviewing past hurts and unfairness is often the place many people start. Looking for the blessings in these seemingly tragic situations is the next step in the soul examination process.

Forgiveness is an essential part of soul examination. It implies not only giving up on the idea that an offense ought to be punished, but also relinquishing any feelings of resentment or vengefulness. Healing at a soul level connects you to people through Spirit. If our desire is to help people heal their souls, we must first release the judgment in ourselves. Depending on the person, forgiving ourselves and others may be easy or difficult, but it is essential for us to have access to Spirit's grace.

When I began my life's work as a massage therapist and energetic healer, I did not need to know much about my clients when they were on the massage table. I could heal them through touch without knowing their 'stories.' As time went on, my clients developed a need to vent and verbally work through what they were experiencing. I found that if I did not check my baggage at the door, meaning my own judgments, either of myself or others, I could not be fully present in my body, and at times I would be pushed completely out or rendered unconscious while channeling a healing.

Before I could stand completely in my power as a multidimensional healer, I had to examine my own soul, which started with forgiving myself. I had to release judgment before I could give advice to others from a clear perspective. I began to have a deeper soul level connection with my clients without the need for touch. I was then able to remain in my body and be present during the channeling and healing parts of our sessions.

Soul examination is a personal journey of uncovering who we are at the spiritual level. It can be amazing, joyful and even exciting. We are free to utilize any and all methods that feel comfortable and right including massage therapy, aromatherapy, taking up a new art form, astrology, energy healing, meditation, or whatever else that helps us heal and strengthen our connection to Source.

Small steps in soul examination will give us meaningful results. However, those who wish to move to the next level of soul healing will need to work at multiple levels. Quite frequently, choosing this path requires significant life changes which can be difficult. When we invite Spirit to join us in our healing, we raise our energetic frequency making these changes softer and gentler. When we are able to clear our baggage through forgiveness, we can expand and channel more of our soul's energy into our physical bodies. Miracles happen every day in our world when we use our opportunity to heal on multiple levels.

Soul examination is driven by our conscious desire to reconnect with Source. We do this by clearing out those aspects of our lives that are not aligned with our soul's purpose. I believe that for most of us, that includes living our lives in the highest level of integrity, clearing our energy fields, releasing judgment, and forgiving ourselves.

CHAPTER SEVEN

Multidimensional Healing

"As you work on yourselves, you are helping everyone and everything else in existence. As you heal your old wounds, limitations and cycles of behavior, you open the doorway for others to find their own path for healing."
~Master Saint Germain

We all come into the physical plane with challenges that need to be acknowledged and healed. The process of **Multidimensional Healing** is an incremental unfolding of levels of consciousness. Similar to peeling the layers of an onion, we open up our energy systems and allow higher levels of awareness to pour in. It is healing on all dimensions at the Soul level.

We may perceive multidimensional healing to be a complex concept. In fact, once broken down to its various components, it is simple and workable. I am not saying that it is easy, but it can be done, as I have observed with hundreds of people. When healing takes place at an energetic or soul level, our hearts, minds and physical bodies immediately notice a difference. Distorted patterns of energy can be cleared and restored to their authentic true templates. The complication lies in the emotional triggers for the ego structure. The analyzing and re-hashing of our past experiences can take some people years to release, or for others, just moments. It all depends on our paths, choices, services in life, and our understanding of the relevancy of these experiences.

When beginning a multidimensional healing process, it is always a good idea to start with a medical assessment to identify or rule out any physical condition that needs to be addressed. I believe that the value of the medical profession is to identify issues on the physical level that may need attention. When a client comes to see me with a physical ailment or concern, one of the first things I suggest is to get a blood test so we can have tangible evidence of where to start. For example, if a blood test reveals that a person has high blood sugar, then we know that diet and exercise will be included in the healing plan. We can then move on to the next level of healing. Everyone has their own timeline and unique process for healing.

When issues of illness, emotional distress or psychological disturbance occur in our lives, multidimensional healing looks at the core or soul causes. Energetic shifts triggered as a result of multidimensional healing can lead to changes surrounding these issues. There is an imprint, or scarring left behind when we are imbalanced due to emotional trauma, wounding, injuries due to accidents in this life, or in another life. Our cells hold memory and this can affect our responses and behavior. These trapped energy patterns can be part of our DNA, familial, cultural, past life experiences or embedded in our spiritual blueprint. When multidimensional healing retrieves the information about the lesson, purpose or meaning of the situation that created the imbalance, the whole story is allowed to unfold, including the other players, whether past, present or future. Then we are able to heal on all levels, physically, emotionally, mentally, spiritually…multidimensionally!

When soul or multidimensional healing happens, it affects our mind, body and emotions in a positive and all-inclusive way. Over the centuries, people from many cultures have used different forms of multidimensional healing, such as trance-like states of meditation, shamanic journeying, prayer and vision quests. Some civilizations have used various forms of movement, like Tai Chi, yoga, walking a labyrinth or dancing. Sound is also a form of healing, including singing, toning, chanting and drumming. Our souls are made of energy. All of the above listed healing modalities will heighten our awareness so that they can assist our energy patterns to shift naturally to a higher frequency.

On the individual level, we can turn to our disciplines and spiritual practices, which may include meditation, fasting, cleansing, and spending time in nature. And, that may be all we need. There will be times when other forms of healing such as energy balancing, acupuncture, massage or herbs, used in combinations, will do the job. Other types of multidimensional healing, such as past life regression and intuitive readings can be beneficial when we are ready to heal with more intensity. Sometimes we may need to turn ourselves over to Source and put our trust in Divine timing. Ultimately, it is our personal responsibility to create a treatment plan that feels safe, and deals with our issues holistically.

When we are genuinely threatened by situations we do not understand, we make choices under duress that impact our belief systems and methods of behavior for our survival. We make rules for ourselves, and teach our children from these places of fear, to protect ourselves and others we care about, so that we may better survive life-threatening situations. These old patterns, when applied to our current life circumstances, may not warrant this type of response, and may not work with our present day lives. What were once survival skills may actually become blocks to what we want or need to evolve and grow. They may no longer serve us in our present environment. However, we may be so afraid of letting go of these old templates, we fear we may literally die.

John came to me with anger issues. In his words, he was "flying off the handle." It was affecting his personal relationships and his job. During a soul retrieval session, John remembered that he had watched his father use his furious temper to manipulate people. Unconsciously, John had adopted his father's habit. He began to see that his behavior did not work in new life situations. He even found that it prevented him from solving his problems, and actually created new ones. Even though it was clear that his formula no longer worked, his mind believed that it was essential to his survival. Over time, John saw that this dynamic was not even his. He was able to see the pattern, isolate it and flush it out, replacing it with an authentic soul piece.

Have you ever heard yourself state a belief that put you off guard? Have you said to yourself "Where did that come from?" Perhaps it was not until you repeated the statement in your head several times that you could hear it in a voice that was not even yours. Maybe it was something your mother, father or a teacher used to say, and it stuck with you. You took it on as your own without even consciously putting it in your belief system. For example: "Money doesn't grow on trees," or "If it's worth having, it's hard work" or "If it was easy everyone would be doing it.' As children, we absorb these declarations; they become our beliefs, and are some of the blocks we find ourselves confronting on our own paths to healing.

Over time, and based on the history of our lives, we develop an ego structure that constructs a limited experience of our true self. With each event we perceive as negative, we create more thoughts, and trigger more feelings of separation. When I work with someone to identify and release the limited self, we start with recognizable areas such as beliefs, emotional states or physical ailments. As healing and release happens, a greater sense of connectedness to Divine Spirit becomes available. The person's soul essence begins to pulse through body and mind, and emotions become more clear. In connected states, it is possible to invoke any quality of being, any state of mind or any action from Divine Source.

In past lives we have lived in many cultures, have followed many religions, lived as different races and sexes. Beliefs that have been with us for many lives at a soul or cellular level may have an accumulation of blocks in our energy field that we desire to release. By pressing into the fear and getting to the soul's truth about the belief, formula or mode for living, we can gain valuable knowledge that can bring healing to those areas where the information was stored, whether in our physical body, an energetic system, or spiritual blueprint.

Michelle began her multidimensional healing process at age twenty-five when she entered traditional psychotherapy. She retrieved many displaced parts of her soul, but felt that she needed more. She began having regular massage treatments, which released trapped energy in her physical body. She explored acupuncture, aromatherapy, and journaling. Eventually she came to see me for energetic healing. I provided channeled information that helped her choose her next life steps. Michelle sees multidimensional healing as a lifestyle, and intends to benefit from it all her life.

I have worked with clients who have had abandonment, rejection and abuse histories of all types. They were able to take their experiences and see strengths that they developed as a result of these traumas. With this awareness, they were able to value the beneficial aspects of their experiences and view them as positive attributes, rather than the negative blemishes they had previously perceived them to be. They could turn around and counsel others going through a similar experience. Sometimes they discovered that the traumas in their lives actually defined their soul's purpose. When this happens, it can feel like it was all worthwhile. When we release blocks and repetitive thoughts, and the 'story' we have been unconsciously carrying, we no longer hold resistance to it and are able to see our soul's truth behind it all. We can learn about the larger purpose behind the event or situation, and heal our souls on all dimensions.

One of the ultimate aspects of multidimensional healing is the retrieval of those parts of our soul that have been split apart, trapped, torn or repressed at the time of a trauma. Some of these dislodged life pieces may hold or block aspects of well-being, love, passion, happiness, as well as offer pathways to Soul's wisdom, mastery and skill. Other lost pieces of our selves may carry unique abilities and talents that would enhance our life experiences. These displaced parts of our soul may have been replaced with artificial formulas and models for living. We no longer have direct communication with our soul's truth, instead allowing these fabricated belief systems to control our subsequent life perceptions, and therefore choices.

There is, literally, no trauma that is too horrendous for the Divine Spirit to heal. As the Masters have told me: "Tapping into that expanded consciousness transcends the whole paradigm of mind, body and emotion, which is considered the sum total of our existence. In a moment, you can create joy or sadness, stand on something important to you or change a lifelong habit. You can create *anything*."

Clearing old energy from our pathways can put us into a type of shock. I have seen clients fall unconscious during and after a re-patterning session. We can also deny and repress bits of a healing process, with the understanding that they can be explored later. When you are clearing old energy pathways, trust that you are all right. Just breathe and understand that you are where you are supposed to be. Sometimes we need to get knocked out of our comfort zone, which may feel overwhelming and exhausting. Try to focus upon the goal and the reward of having the life you long for. Once the fog has cleared, we will have the clarity we need to see things we may have missed earlier. By releasing old, non-serving patterns and beliefs on all levels, we have the ability to choose differently next time. We can use this contrast to compare our past experiences to what is actually desired in our current life.

Not all life experiences or injuries are meant to be healed. Some situations have been created to be overcome, while other conditions were created for us to live with as part of our life's teaching. Finding out what we can change and what we are meant to live with can take up a huge part of our lives, or can be understood at an early age. It all depends on our level of acceptance and our willingness or ability to surrender to the process of learning. Life's teachings are not always brought to us in the form of unpleasant or upsetting situations. These events can happen during extremely passionate and happy moments as well. Until we learn to surrender and develop faith in the process, they will often be challenging.

Healing does not always mean that the person's physical body heals. Healing can mean that the person has released negative thoughts, that belief systems have shifted, or that the lessons associated with the illness have been received. A person may choose to spend their remaining energy wrapping things up, so they are ready to go on to their next assignment.

I had a client who came to me when he was dealing with his second bout of cancer, a type of leukemia, which had been in remission for years. Going through chemotherapy and trying to present a confident face for his family and friends, he kept saying that he was still in a fight with the disease. When I read his energy, I saw that he had actually given up. After about three sessions, he finally admitted that he did not think he could win the battle and that, instead, he was in need of help to manage pain and plan a graceful exit. I did energy work on him, and supplied him with skills for dealing with pain. He eventually made a decision to end the medical therapy, whose side effects were taking away from his quality of life. In essence, he made a conscious choice to allow his life to end, and focused his energy on any spiritual situations that had unfinished business.

I believe that we, with the help of our spiritual counselors, created blueprints for our lives before we came into being. These blueprints listed the things we wished to personally heal, learn from and possibly teach, for the purpose of healing our selves and our planet. We also contracted a way of bringing in or magnifying obstacles or injuries for the process of learning and healing. Do not tear them away or brush them aside. There may be vast knowledge tucked away within these challenging situations for us to harvest.

We enter this dimension, or physical existence, with a spiritual blueprint that contains our lessons for this incarnation. Serious physical impairments and/or mental illnesses are an ongoing lesson for some people. These people may not be contracted to heal physically in their lifetime. These souls, and others influenced by them, can still benefit from the lessons encoded in their blueprints, and work on areas that can be healed. It is important that we connect and really communicate with our souls about this until we feel clear about what can be healed and what must be lived with. This process can be used to create the template we use to heal areas of our next life.

I like to refer to the remarkable story of Christopher Reeve, the actor who portrayed Superman in the 1978 film and sequels. In 1995, he fell off a horse and sustained a cervical spinal injury that left him paralyzed from the neck down. The ironic event that disabled Superman and put him in a wheelchair was transformed into a teaching that touched so many lives. Since he was covered constantly by the press, he used his celebrity to promote awareness of spinal cord injuries. He was able to raise money for stem cell research, and continued to act, direct and produce movies until his death, at age fifty two. Even though he died young, he had a great impact on the world. These types of situations can become part of our soul's journey and purpose.

I believe that we come into physical form to experience all emotions. It is in this contrast of pain and happiness that we can compare and make informed decisions about what we really want or what is highest and best for us. To start this process, the most challenging change will be how we view all of our feelings, especially the painful ones.

We are divided into opposites: male and female, dark and light, good and bad. We are here to rectify our dualistic natures. There is no bad or evil other than that which we create for ourselves based on our beliefs. Source does not judge us as good or bad. We are the ones, who assign meaning to the circumstances that surround us. This is true for illness and disease as well. When we accept, learn the lesson from and integrate our physical ailments, we can move through them.

From this perspective, depression may be a signal from our souls or higher selves that something needs to be looked at, reorganized or shifted. It is a call for a spiritual house cleaning, not a huge emotional ordeal to be avoided. Sadness, depression and fear are just a few of the messages that come to us, giving us the opportunity to learn and make new informed decisions.

In our modern society, so many people use medication to manage their emotions. In my work, I have helped many clients to gradually, under doctor's care, discontinue the use of psychiatric medication. For the most part, these are people who are dealing with grief, death of loved ones, financial stress, divorce and all types of significant losses. What these challenging times have in common is that they contain the condition of managing sudden change. Many of us have lost the ability to remember how to cope, grow and advance from these difficult periods of our lives. We are not unfortunate victims, having these unpleasant life occurrences imposed upon us. I see them as the yin to happiness's yang. When we accept that not all emotions are pleasant, we can achieve the balance that feeling all emotions delivers.

We, as creatures that contain both light and dark, must process our negative or dark emotions as well as the positive or light ones. When we understand that we are the creators of our world, we learn from and integrate our dark sides. Information, skill and strength can be harvested from our shadows. When transmuted and integrated, they can be useful in becoming balanced and whole. The intention is to lift the cycles of non-functioning emotional patterns and open space to create what your soul truly wants from this life.

Another form of multidimensional healing is to take advantage of our relationship with our Spirit Guides, Angels and Ascended Master Teachers. Spirit Guides may be ancestors of our current incarnation, souls from past lives, or beings from in-between states that we have contracted with in this lifetime. Angels and Ascended Master Teachers may be considered Spirit Guides as well. Some are only with us for important or critical life events, and others are with us for a lifetime or longer. In my experience, each person is flanked by at least two Spirit Guides at all times, and at least one is an Angel. Depending on what we are going through or working on, we may have more around us at any given time.

Depending on our life lessons and themes, our Spirit Guides, Angels and Ascended Master Teachers may allow or create situations that require us to stick to our original spiritual blueprint. A good starting place is to acknowledge that they happen for our learning and growth. These occurrences are strategically delivered at the perfect time to give us opportunities to focus our attention on addressing the issues. Otherwise, they will continue to show up until we have the willingness to see them through. As we get more proficient at spotting issues as they surface, they will arrive a bit more gently, and we will be able to head them off before they become painful, costly or life threatening. The goal is to heal our issues before they manifest in the physical realm.

An example from my personal life is when I asked *My Team* of Spirit Guides, Angels and Ascended Master Teachers if it was highest and best for me to revisit an old relationship that did not work out the first time. The answer I received was *"Yes."* It was a rocky road that ended abruptly. When I asked them why they would give me a green light on a situation that was so painful, they replied, *"There was something that you did not understand the first time around. The second time you understood."* Going back and resolving the issues from this relationship helped me complete my karmic lesson. I am not planning on manifesting that relationship dynamic again!

Today, with the aid of my *My Team*, I am definitely on a need-to-know basis, which means that I *do not* need to know or understand everything that is going on at any particular time. I am comfortable just knowing that my job is to show up, do what I do, and trust that the people, places and things I need will be there to support me. In fact, I am constantly reminded by *My Team* that the how and why are none of my business. I know and trust that nothing happens by accident.

The condition of our bodies and life circumstances are a reflection of our thoughts and actions, and are indicators of what needs to be worked on. When we surrender to the process, we have faith, and turn the heavy lifting over to our soul council or team. We will have less resistance around the change that is required of us. When a shift takes place, we will see the blessings in the big picture of our life, understand our teaching and clear the confusion.

All of our answers lie deep inside of us, below the surface of our patterns and protective belief systems. What most of us do not realize or comprehend, as we tackle the mysteries of healing ourselves, is that as we do so, we are helping everyone and everything in existence. As we heal our wounds, limitations and cycles of behavior, we open the doorway for others to find their own paths to healing.

We are all linked through a vast web which connects life at an atomic level. Science has discovered that even at the smallest cellular level, our bodies hold memory. The energy grid or network that sustains all life has many tiny connections. It is the spiritual highway that I tap into when I heal, whether it includes hands-on work, or even long distance healing. Without this cellular or atomic level connection, I would not be able to receive direction from the Masters or send healing energy to my clients. I am simply the conscious connector. I help others be aware of and expand their already existing connection to this web of awareness, or spiritual highway.

We need to surrender to the healing process our soul has laid out for us. At the soul level we are whole, aware and connected with Source and our blueprint in this lifetime. Each of us are limitless beings of light and awareness. This is an important time to integrate the highest soul level frequencies we can.

We, as a culture and as individuals, are going through an immense process of eradication of old beliefs and patterns. At the same time we are also manifesting new and improved ones. Sickness, lack, and fear can be fully released once we observe, press into, understand, heal, resolve and clear old energy patterns. As we heal our own ego-defined self-limiting misconceptions that have held us hostage, the ramifications of our individual healing will assist mass consciousness in shifting to higher frequencies as well. When a human being gets to the point where they experience themselves as Divine Spirit, the outcome is reverence for all humanity.

CHAPTER EIGHT

Energetic Pathways

"Your energy systems are the spiritual counterpart to your physiology. They are the underlying foundation of your body."
~Master Djwal Khul

The human energy system is complex and made up of many sub-systems. Human energetic pathways channel the soul's energy in, around and through these systems in our bodies. Energetic pathways carry the life force and bring information in the form of light, sound, and the activation of all our senses. They also bring in energy from the world around us and connect us to Source when we are in heightened states of being.

We learn about the physical systems of the body, and symptoms of our illnesses in order to understand and heal disease on the physical plane. Similarly, understanding how our energetic systems work together can provide us with the tools we need to navigate healing on the spiritual plane. Once we are aware of these systems, we can create a stronger connection to Source. When our energy pathways are clear, our soul's messages can be received and acknowledged more effectively. We may choose to concentrate on one system, and as our understanding grows, we may use all of them interchangeably as needed. These techniques can then be used for healing our spirit, which is reflected in the health of our bodies.

To fully comprehend energetic pathways could take lifetimes to investigate and study. There are many exceptional books out there on the subject of the different energy systems. In this chapter, I will briefly discuss a few of the fundamental systems, networks and energy pathways I work with in my healing practice. These systems are not unique to me. In fact, healers through the ages have tapped into the same energy pathways by different names.

Soul energies enter us from Source where they are channeled into the physical body through our chakra column, starting at the crown of our heads. From there, they flow out to the subtle bodies, creating an auric field. At the same time, they illuminate our auric matrix, fill our meridians and establish the kundalini pathway up the spine, and ultimately flow down into the core of the earth. In this way, all living things are the connectors that transmit the continual flow of energy between Father/Source and Mother/Earth.

The *Aura* is kindred to what the scientists call the electromagnetic field around our bodies. It is oval or egg-shaped and moves and changes as we do. It defines our personal space and fluctuates, depending on what we are experiencing in any given moment. On average it extends eighteen inches to three feet around the body. We are continually transmitting and processing knowledge and data from our environment through this human atmosphere or auric field.

With our dualistic nature at present, male and female fields vary, with male auric fields being mostly electric, and female being mostly magnetic. Women unconsciously draw things into their field from the environment while men send out intensely charged energy. When we learn to work with our energy more effectively, we can learn to deflect the flow of negative or unwanted energy, and expand our ability to attract positive or useful energies. Consciously or unconsciously, others are aware of what kind of energy we radiate. Therefore, it serves humanity to emanate positive and loving energy. If we are consciously working at using our energies, we can learn to draw to us whatever we desire, shift the energy dynamic of any situation and create healthy energetic boundaries.

It is important to balance the energies within ourselves and learn to use them when we interact with our world. We, as enlightened beings, have a responsibility to teach by our example. If you're going to answer the phone, be willing to have a conversation at the highest energetic level you can. Just as we look at our reflection in the mirror before we leave the house, we can also check our energy before we interact with others.

When I see a person's aura it is like fluid colors that are constantly wavering. Other living things and objects also have auras. Auras can change color and shape when an individual is interacting with others. They may be one or more predominate color, depending on our mood, or what we are going through at the time. Due to their electric nature, the auric fields of men are sometimes larger than those of women, who are naturally magnetic. I can see if there is an imbalance in a person's auric field, such as an illness or strong emotion. When I look at someone, I see the colors of the emotional body first and most clearly.

There are many layers to the auric field. I will be introducing four of the most recognizable *Subtle Body Layers,* called the **etheric, emotional, mental** and **spiritual bodies.** The subtle body layers each act as a representation, expression or characteristic of ourselves; they overlap and surround each other in successive layers.

The layer closest to our physical body is the ***Etheric Body***. It extends approximately six inches around the body, and is a slightly expanded version of our physical body. It has also been called the *luminous, vital* or *astral* body. The etheric body surrounds and sustains our physical being. Organ for organ and molecule for molecule, it is the exact three-dimensional counterpart of our physical body. It reveals each organ, internal system, only larger, just above the body from where it is located. For instance, the heart is several inches larger and hovers above the physical heart.

Injury, illness or damage shows up in the etheric body first, where it stores mental and emotional imprints as cellular memory. The physical body gets this information from the etheric body and then directs the regeneration of cells accordingly. Unexplained ailments may manifest in our bodies through our etheric body from past life wounds, death experiences or unresolved lessons. When we heal our etheric bodies, we can then integrate new patterns that are balanced and whole. From this new energy level, we can form cells for our bodies that are healthy. Energetic healing can heal the etheric body in a matter of moments before there is even a physical symptom.

The ***Emotional Body*** is the next layer of the aura. It starts about four to six inches from the etheric body and surrounds and extends from the body approximately twelve to eighteen inches. This is the most easily seen subtle body. It is most visible to clairvoyants who see color and movement, which can change with our emotions. The emotional body interprets incoming energy as feelings based on the perspective we have created with our beliefs and thoughts. Love, fear, anger and happiness are all first experienced in the emotional body. External stimuli trigger our emotions to create our moods. Our in-completions, suppressed emotions or imprints from painful past life experiences are also stored in the emotional body.

When we get triggered emotionally, or our buttons get

pushed, these little dots of energy get pressed and expand so that we can re-experience stored memories as if they are in present time, with all the emotions and physical sensations attached. For example, old sibling rivalry disputes, if triggered as adults, can send us right back to the emotions of being six years old during a confrontation. Once we are aware of these old emotional buttons, healing can take place, and they can be released.

The ***Mental Body*** is the next layer of the aura, which starts just beyond the emotional body. It is where our cognition, knowing, comprehension, reasoning and discernment reside. Our beliefs, concepts, patterns, formulas and contracts are stored in the mental body. We can get stuck if we are running outdated mental programs based on survival issues, for example, stress over money or not having a safe home. These templates, behaviors or models for living helped us to survive in the past, which can make it difficult for us to release them, even when the threat may be gone. It is as if we are still stuck in a limited survival mode. We may still be responding and reacting to new stimuli out of fear through these old programs. They can end up being the blocks that prevent us from moving forward.

Once the habitual brain patterns and filters have been removed, we are able to respond to situations from the present moment, be more creative and have an abundance of choices. We can then trust the information that we are receiving and have clear communication with Spirit.

The ***Spirit Body*** is the last and outer layer of the auric field. It is also referred to as the *celestial body*. This is where we can have contact and interact directly with our Spirit Guides, Angels and Ascended Master Teachers. By using deep meditation, we can interface our energy with theirs, and feel Divine love fully and clearly. In the spirit body, communication comes to us as light particles and energy waves that are interpreted and broken down into emotions, images and information that is distributed through our other subtle bodies and energy systems.

The *Hara Line* is our energetic connection to Father Source (above) and Mother Earth (below). It is like a pillar or column that runs vertically through the human body starting at the head and down into the core of the planet. In order to center our awareness on ourselves, we can focus on this connection. Due to the fact that it is a zero-point energy field, it is a place of deep calm.

The Hara Line is divided into three sections. The top is referred to as the *source connection*, the middle part is referred to as the *chakra column* and the bottom part is referred to as the *grounding cord*. These three parts work together or independently depending on where or what we are focused on.

The *Source Connection*, which we have discussed in previous chapters, is channeled through the top of the head through the seventh chakra. It links us to the vast expanse of universal God energy and *All That Is*.

Chakra means *turning wheel* in Sanskrit, and in the yogic context it means vortex or whirlpool. Chakras sometimes appear as lotus flowers. The number of petals may vary, depending on the chakra location. At other times, they appear as spinning, swirling wheels of energy that open and close like a camera lens. When we send energy out through the chakras, the energy moves in a clockwise motion, and when we draw energy into our chakras, the energy moves in a counter-clockwise motion. The clockwise direction balances and builds energy, while counter-clockwise direction releases energy. Chakras are the main conduits, or channels, for our soul energy to enter or leave our bodies. The chakras are associated with the rainbow light spectrum of electromagnetic frequencies. They interpret these particles of light into signals that can be transmitted to the central nervous system. The chakras channel vital life force energy for our organs. For example, the heart chakra sends energy to our heart and the surrounding area, the third eye chakra sends energy to the brain and pineal gland, and so on. They supply energy for multiple physiological functions. For instance, when we speak our truth, our throat chakra sends energy to support our voice in the physical body.

The most well-known chakras are the seven major ones, agreed upon by belief systems from many cultures. They are vertically aligned with the spine and are contained in the middle of the Hara Line. There are many different beliefs about how many total chakras we actually have. Some say there are seven, some say nine or thirteen, and I have even heard about a belief system that claims more than one hundred! I have seen or worked with at least twenty three major, minor and chakra-like portals in and around our energy systems. Some pass through the body, some are above, below, to the side or floating in the auric field, while others are only visible or open at certain times. In the last several years I have noticed new energy centers in my student's and client's auric fields. I believe that as we develop and grow, new or dormant chakras are able to open to interpret new information. Everyone's abilities are unique to them, and will change as their perspectives change.

The colors of the chakras may change slightly over the years of our lives, as we change. The chakras and auric fields of each individual are like an energetic fingerprint. The colors, shapes and energy fields shift constantly as we move, think and respond to the stimuli around us in this world, and from other dimensions.

Now to discuss briefly each of the **Seven Major Chakras** independently, as I see them:

The *First,* or root *Chakra,* when healthy, is a clear ruby red and is located at the base of the spine just below our physical body. The first chakra correlates with the adrenal glands, is about four inches in circumference and is shaped like a funnel with the mouth pointed down. The role of this chakra is to house our survival responses around food, shelter and security in the material world. It is also where our beliefs about our identity in this incarnation are stored.

The **Second**, or sacral **Chakra**, is a rich coppery or pumpkin orange when in a healthy state. The second chakra correlates with the ovaries and testes. It holds our sexual energy, guilt, desire and the energy around money and creating abundance. This is the chakra that deals with creativity, passion and relationships. It is where our musician, artist, inventor and writer are birthed. The juicy energy of the second chakra houses our excitement, attraction patterns and physical vigor. How we interact with the outside world depends on the health of our second chakra.

The **Third**, or the solar plexus **Chakra**, is a vibrant golden yellow when it is cleared and healthy. The third chakra correlates to the pancreas and is the seat of our personal power and self-discipline. It is also our intuitive center, where we can discern the truth and pick up information about our environment. Our ego, personality, and self esteem affect, and are affected by, the energies of the third chakra. It is also the seat of the fight-or-flight response (fear), as well as emotions such as shame, anger, and courage. When the third chakra is fully healed, we are able to access our heart chakra and connect to our higher chakras.

The **Fourth**, or heart **Chakra**, is a deep emerald green, or in some a luscious pink. It may look like a pink lotus blossom with green leaves. It is located in the chest near the heart, but more centrally aligned with the spine. The heart chakra correlates to the thymus gland. It is filled with love, compassion, and the ability to forgive loved ones despite the hurts of the past. It is also the center of jealously, envy and unrequited love. A heart chakra open to Divine love can break down walls, build bridges and get us through our darkest times. Only through our hearts can we be true.

The **Fifth**, or throat **Chakra**, is a light silvery or turquoise blue and is located at the base of the neck. This chakra correlates to the thyroid. The energy of this chakra supports us when we speak our truth. This is an important chakra for manifesting our desires in the physical realm, and is used to express our selves verbally. It defines the way we communicate, possibly deceive, judge our selves and others, and interact and voice our messages.

The *Sixth,* or third eye *Chakra,* is a dark indigo or deep purple in color and is located in the center of the head around the pineal gland. This is the psychic or clairvoyant center, where our intuition, nightmares, dreams, and imagination serves us. The sixth chakra carries all the pictures of our current and past lives. These pictures can be vivid and literal, or foggy and symbolic, depending on our level of awareness and perception. This is the very valuable real estate of the frontal lobe. Here we can magically create anything with just a thought, picture or fantasy.

The *Seventh,* or crown *Chakra,* can be purple, lavender or even white in color. It is located at the top of the head and can radiate up to seven inches above the body. This chakra governs many bodily functions, and correlates with the pituitary gland. The seventh chakra is the door to multiple dimensions. We receive Divine love, messages, and energy from Source through the crown chakra. It is our bridge or connection to Source energy and *All That Is*. It is important that we work with the seventh chakra with pure intentions.

Of the many chakras or energy centers we possess, these are the major intersections for this primary energy system. Like pistons in a car motor, the chakras all work together. When one is out of balance it affects all the others, and conversely, healthy chakras help each other stay in balance as well.

There are a few additional chakras that I feel are worth bringing up. We have chakras in our hands and feet for sending and receiving healing energy, and for grounding and connecting with Earth energies. We have chakras above our ears. There is also a chakra in the back of our head between the third eye and crown that has only became noticeable to me in the last few years. I refer to it as the eighth chakra. It is how we channel our soul into our bodies. By accessing a larger volume of our higher selves, it is becoming more functional in my clients and students. I'll discuss these chakras in more detail in Chapter 12.

The lower third of the Hara Line is the **Grounding Cord**, which anchors our soul energy to our body and to the planet. The more grounded we are, the higher or further we can move interdimensionally. When properly connected, the grounding cord fosters a calm and grounded feeling. When we are ungrounded we feel spacey, are unable to concentrate and are easily knocked off center. As we grow and shift, the Hara Line will shift accordingly, accommodating larger or more intense frequencies of energy as they run through our systems. We can also draw earth energy up into ourselves through our grounding cord to heal or manifest on the physical level.

Meridians are pathways of energy that carry life force through the body. This life force has been called many things, including chi, prana, Spirit or Source energy. Meridians are like rivers or streams flowing through our energy systems, revitalizing energy to our organs and physical body. Emotions, injuries, and trauma can create blocks that interrupt the flow of energy, which can lead to a deficiency or excess of energy to the organs. This is the major energy system utilized and treated by an acupuncturist.

There are twelve primary meridian channels running through the body. The points on these channels function as energy reservoirs, which can be opened up with acupuncture needles, pressure or tapping. These points, or valves, regulate the amount of energy traveling through the meridians and can hold, release or receive energy.

The *Matrix* is made up of wispy veils between our subtle

bodies and our other energy systems. It is like a fiber optic web that carries information back and forth from one system to another on little electric bursts or charges. There may be hidden filters in the matrix where information is processed before it gets broken down into bite-sized pieces of information that we can understand. When the matrix is fully functional and repaired, information can travel through our field at lightning speed, connecting all our systems almost at once. In most of us, there are little disconnects or blockages in the webs where energy needs to be re-routed. This is often due to protective systems that have been formed as a result of our non-serving beliefs.

Kundalini is an energy channel originating in the sacrum, or base of the spine. In Sanskrit, Kundalini means *she who is coiled*. It is rendered as female energy lying coiled at the base of the spine, also called serpent power. Its function is to feed and nourish the chakras and other energy systems. A healthy kundalini system will lead to a strong nervous system and physical body. This channel can become quite gummed up from the density of one's karmic body, creating blockages that can lead to disturbing physical and psychic symptoms. Yogic traditions say Kundalini energy can be awakened through meditation, pranayama breathing or by chanting mantras. Some people attempt to create a sense of bliss by focusing the kundalini energy through the upper chakras. This by itself rarely leads to actual awakening.

I had what I now know to be a kundalini awakening. I had been reading, and put my book down to gaze at the light coming in through my patio door. In my relaxed state, I watched prisms of light bounce off a crystal, dance around the room and shine on my face. Mesmerized, I was suddenly hit by a feeling of total bliss, and what felt like a warming sensation in my root chakra and groin area. The light spectrum rainbow crossed the threshold of my eyes and activated my kundalini energy. It spiraled up my spine and out the top of my head. It was like a full body orgasm without the sexual bit. My body involuntarily jerked, tremors and tingles ran through me, and I heard a high-pitched humming in my ears. This lasted a full minute and left me with a feeling of complete joy, a knowing, passion, bliss and a love for all things. Just thinking about that moment sent me into a trance-like state for weeks afterward. I would forget to eat and would get lost in the beauty of simple things for what felt like hours.

Everyone can connect to their energetic pathways and open up to other dimensions and higher frequencies of energy. One way to do this is through meditation. The more you become aware of your own energy systems, the more you will be able to sense when they are out of balance. Regular examination of our energetic pathways through meditation is the best way to remain in synchrony.

When we clean out the debris trapped in our energetic pathways and they begin to function in harmony, we are able to see our karmic challenges more clearly. This insight can be used to reset our karmic clocks. Understanding our energy systems is a powerful step in tracking the patterns that create the symptoms of illness or dis-ease. It is important to trust our intuitive sense, above any teaching, theory or philosophy, including this material. The workbook and meditations available on my website, DarcyCleome.com, offer exercises for those who are interested in developing their skills and taking their journey to the next level.

CHAPTER NINE

Resetting Our Karmic Clocks

"As your consciousness is freed up from your past history, you have more of your soul essence available to experience, help others, and heal the planet."
~Master Kuan Yin

Karma: *(in Hinduism and Buddhism) 1. The force generated by a person's actions in this and previous states of existence, viewed as determining the nature of the person's future existences. 2. Destiny or fate following as effect from cause.*

Karma has been thought of as a punishment, reward, or balance of actions and reactions. Well, yes and so much more! Karma represents our life themes, lessons, patterns of behavior and unfinished business that show up for us to review, sometimes relive, heal and hopefully release. Karma can be defined as our spiritual blueprint. In fact, throughout this book we have actually been discussing karma all along.

All of us have karmic themes, lessons and ongoing business

that come up for us at different times. These lessons can be inside of, coincide with, or overlap different phases of our lives. We may have personal or shared beliefs that create blocks to our personal power and wealth, or we may be stuck in racial or religious prejudices. These karmic themes are part of the evolution of mass consciousness awakening.

Most of us are not living in isolation and solitude. Our connection with others and the outside world will, at some point, cause us to face challenging mental processes, emotional byproducts from relationships, and undesired life experiences. In order to reach and maintain higher states of consciousness, we have to clear out lower frequency patterns, beliefs, and filtering systems created by our past. Much of the time, our minds are dwelling on the past or speculating about the future. It is like those old sayings, 'You can't get there from here' or 'You can't create something new from the same frequency you have been creating at.' These musings are based on past experiences, which cause us to re-create future experiences from that same old space.

When a client comes to me seeking help with finding fulfillment in their life, I believe that their karma is present. I start by asking certain questions: What do you enjoy doing, what are your hobbies? What makes your heart sing? Putting aside what you might be educated or trained to do, and if money was not an obstacle, what would put a smile on your face when you're doing it? What makes time fly? What makes you feel passionate? Possibly, the most significant question I ask is, "When did you stop dancing (literally or metaphorically)? When the client replies with a recollection of an event or life experience, I follow it with, "That is the day you decided to be less than who you are." This simple reminder is often a very emotional and tearful realization, and is a powerful means for reconnecting us to who we are.

The responses I hear to my inquiries are often preceded by an apprehensive giggle or mannerism. The words that accompany these behaviors are nearly always along these lines. "Oh, I can't make a real living doing that…" or "Who is going to pay me to do that?" The most common theme is "Well, that's not very practical or responsible." My absolute favorite is, "Who would even want what I have to offer?"

These are excellent examples of the kind of fear-based, repetitive thought patterns that manifest as a result of our karmic conditioning. Once we speak our fears out loud, we usually realize that our beliefs have been given to us by people, experiences and negative impressions from our past and present journeys. We have free will to identify them as 'not mine' and make a decision to let them go. This frees us to imagine that we can be who we want to be and to accept new possibilities in our world view.

As you start to clear your karma, you may find aspects of your life start to change and unravel. In the clearing of your karma you will eventually be able to see your soul's purpose. If you can manage to avoid creating new karma, then anything is possible!

At times, we may feel that the paths that lead us to raise our frequency are painful and slow. Be patient, and trust the Divine timeline that has been created just for you. It takes practice to break old habits and replace outdated belief patterns with new ones. For most of us, it is important to learn how to retrieve our expansive collection of knowledge while also living a normal life, as we see it. It is our desire to have a deeper connection to Source that gives us the courage to face theses challenges. The gifts of our soul's experience can help us grow and evolve, and make a difference in anchoring positive energy in this world, which is greatly needed.

Our personal blueprint for this life will make sense when our life themes surface for us to observe. When we find ourselves replaying our life lessons again and again, they become more visible, and can be explored in greater detail with mental and cellular memory sensations. We may even bring a talent into this life from a past life, or understand a relationship with someone we have karma with. Through the spirit body we can discover, examine and heal our past, or let go of anything we would like to release.

I discovered I had past life karma with my son Weston when I was doing energy work on him one day. It was as if a movie started playing in my mind's eye of a past life we had shared. The mental movie brought to light who we were, the themes and roles we played in each other's lives, and also the lesson for both of us in that lifetime. It revealed a lesson that he and I were still working on in this lifetime.

As I narrated the scene, he surprised me by adding information that only the soul from his past life would know. It was as if we were watching the movie together. At the time, I had never shared a past life memory with someone I knew in this lifetime. He added details like his age, name, the year of the event we both recalled, and the lesson we were there to learn, through his perspective.

After the session with him, I was very excited and was discussing what had just happened. Weston had no recollection of what he had said during the session and didn't even remember saying anything. This was one of those times when I wished I had recorded it, but there was just no way I could have foreseen that something like this would happen. Even though this information came directly through him, I suspect that he was not ready to consciously integrate it at that time. Since then, he has remembered bits and pieces, and we have cleared the karma we shared together associated with that past life.

Let us briefly discuss how karma, or an issue that pushes our buttons, moves through the subtle body layers. Karmic patterns can show up in any energy system. Someone may have a chronic pain in their lower back, but no memory of being injured in this lifetime. It could be a karmic issue manifesting in the first or second chakra, or even a past life imprint manifesting in this life's physical body, that also shows up in the etheric body. If karmic themes are not addressed in the spirit body (the outermost layer), they will move towards the core through the mental, emotional, and etheric bodies. For instance, if someone is having issues with addiction in the mental body, it may present itself as a conversation with someone about addiction, meeting someone who is battling addiction, or having thoughts of their own addiction. If not dealt with in the mental body, the theme could then move on to the emotional body. This person may begin having emotions about addiction, or dream about it. In the physical body it could show up as acting out an addiction.

When our life's purpose is ignored, rejected or not realized, the person's soul and team of Spiritual Guides will create and/or allow disturbances in our lives. These can manifest as tragedy, loss, or affliction that create a tear in the fabric of our subtle body layers. At some point these situations will require confrontation, if not in this lifetime, then in another lifetime or reality. Our soul's evolution is to become more aware of the signs of these orchestrated events, and learn how to deal with them effectively, so that we may raise our energetic frequency. We are here to learn these complex lessons concerning cause and effect. Nowhere is the schooling more clear than in the physical realm.

The patterns and events in our lives can be the 'wake up' calls that give us the opportunity to view our repetitive cycles of behavior for what they truly are. Sometimes the messages sent by our subtle bodies are not seen or acknowledged consciously. Sometimes our comfortable holding patterns, fear of change, or other cycles of behavior, block us from living fully as our authentic selves. When we learn to identify the patterns as they surface and heal them, we will not have to re-live them again or bring them into our physical life experience.

We can compare the energy systems of the body to a home that is being rewired to receive a higher level of energy. In order to do this, old wiring must be removed and replaced with the higher grade. In our bodies, we can change out old programs and upgrade them in many ways, such as improving our diet, practicing meditation, or receiving energy healing work. In this way, we rewire our systems to raise our capacity to receive more complex information from Source.

There are many lessons that we have brought into this life to be evaluated and balanced. Our karma, or spiritual blueprint, influences our choices in parents and family, geographic locations, birth and childhood circumstances. Our relationships, personal drama, and issues from childhood, religion, and culture continuously manifest as karmic themes for us to work through.

The purpose of these themes is to rise above the duality or conflict and be loving, have faith, and use our strengths in a spiritual way. This challenge can be immediate and sudden for some, and painstakingly meticulous for others, depending on our personal healing path.

Channel: *1. An electric circuit that acts as a path for a signal. 2. Frequency spectrum used in transmission. 3. A medium for communication or the passage of information. 4. A person who acts as a conduit or medium for a spirit.*

Akashic: Hindu word of Sanskrit origin meaning etheric. This information is available in the Library of Akashic Records These records hold the imprints of every moment in time. Every event, thought and feeling in existence is recorded in the Akashic records, sometimes referred to as The Library.

The Akashic records contain our spiritual blueprint, including a list of karmic challenges to be addressed in our present lifetime. It is like a template, or guide, for every soul's life plan. Also recorded are our personal challenges, beliefs, experiences and relationships. These records are in the spirit body and can be accessed by raising our own energy levels, asking for help from our Spirit Guides, Angels and Ascended Master Teachers, or consulting with a psychic or clairvoyant, who can channel the information for you. Through our soul's connection to Source, we have access to everything that ever was or will be.

By working with a reliable channel, we can relive a story and experience it from a relaxed, meditative state of being. This is a good time to retrieve soul parts from past life experiences that were left behind, heal them, and reincorporate or integrate them back into our energy fields. Not everyone is ready to access information this way. Using an intuitive channel you trust is one of many ways we can learn about out karmic legacy.

There is a difference between being an intuitive or medium, and physically channeling a spirit being. The first is relaying information that I hear, see, smell, taste, or feel. The other is allowing my body to be used as a bio-suit by another, like a cosmic hitchhiker. When this happens, the spirit being experiences all my body senses, while my own consciousness steps back and to the right.

Benjamin felt the need for some reflective time in retreat and was on a road trip. He stopped in town for a cup of coffee and a much-needed leg stretch. An available parking space showed up for him in front of Amethyst Healing Center. As he pulled in, he noticed our sign for intuitive reading and spiritual counseling.

About a month prior, Benjamin's life partner, Steve, had died. Benjamin was in the process of trying to find out who he wanted to be as a single person. During our session, Steve's spirit came through me and gave Benjamin permission to sell his collections, car and other personal items. Most of all, he let Benjamin know that it was alright for him to move on. Also, the spirit of a woman named Mary that had known Benjamin in a past life came to the reading. Mary had a Mae West type of persona, and was very extravagant in her consolation of him, calling him "Kitten." I do not make it a common practice to have physical contact with my clients during sessions, but because I was channeling Mary's soul essence, I was not completely aware of what she doing with my body. When I finished the session, I found myself holding Benjamin and stroking his hair.

Now, a little channeling humor here! This is one of those 'How to recover gracefully in an unusual setting' dilemmas. I remember thinking, "Oh my goodness, what am I doing?" This is why I would caution others who are curious or interested in channeling. Channeling is actually a form of possession of the physical body by another spirit. Opening a gate to any spirit or energy is risky and potentially dangerous. *My Team* helps me determine if channeling a spirit is safe, and if it is the highest and best way in assisting with the healing of another. I would never put myself or my client at risk by allowing a lower frequency entity to enter my body.

After the session, Benjamin told me that he knew that Mary was his soul mate, although he had not met her in this lifetime. Mary was very nurturing and compassionate with Benjamin over his recent loss. Since his first visit with me, Benjamin has had other communication with both Steve and Mary and has learned to access his own multidimensional healing abilities. As a result, he made changes in his life and is using his knowledge to help others. We were glad to welcome him to our collective at Amethyst Healing Center.

My first experience as a channel of a spirit being was when I had a booth set up at a Wellness Clinic where doctors, hospital administrators and pharmacists were discussing the latest available procedures and drugs. My frustration level was rising because, to me, it seemed as though this was an *Illness* Clinic, where they were promoting illness as opposed to health. The accepted philosophy appeared to be that you *will* get sick and this is what we can do to fix you. At some point, I voiced this to several people at my booth and was overheard by the woman who had organized the event.

She approached me and commented that I needed to get up on the stage (following the head surgeon of a local hospital) and give my viewpoint. Fear gripped me! I could not see how I might contribute on a level that matched the doctor's medical expertise. She did not give me an option and said that she was putting me on the schedule. I headed to the bathroom where I turned a vacant stall into a place of communication with *My Team*. Since they had directed me here, I asked them for help to get me through it.

I got up on the stage with the thought that I would just introduce myself and talk about Amethyst Healing Center. Starting with a statement about wellness, I was suddenly booted out of my body and to the right of it. My Spirit Guide, Mr. R., had taken me over. I recognized his personality as he talked to this group of medically-minded individuals. The best way to describe my condition is the drowsy, floating feeling of coming out of anesthesia where I could hear but was visually impaired. In this state, I was not too concerned until I heard myself say something about 'Christ Consciousness,' and my mind panicked. This was NOT the group to address that way! I popped back in, which let me know that it was possible to re-enter my body if I desired. After a long pause, I decided that I was not as capable as he, and allowed him to continue.

Mr. R. returned to his talk, and it was not until he finished that I found myself back in my body. I managed, "Thank you, very much." and walked off the stage. When I returned to my booth, friends confirmed that they had seen the transformation and one person even commented that my voice was not my own. According to others, Mr. R. had spoken about holding the vibrational frequency of health and well being, and switching the focus to these conditions instead of the negative frequency of disease. In other words, he promoted preventative, holistic medicine as an alternative to the medical diagnosis and treatment of symptoms.

This exciting and new way *My Team* shared their energy through me was monumental. I knew that they could express whatever needed to be given for any situation, and it created a great sense of support and love. My confidence in what I could accomplish soared, and I realized that we had taken our relationship to a completely new level. At the same time, I was in awe of what I had been shown.

Seth came to see me because of unresolved feelings he had due to the death of his father as a young boy. By viewing the experience together, Seth was able to relive that time without the pain, and observe the experiences that altered his life perceptions. In doing this, he could see how it affected his abilities to parent his children, share closeness with others, and enjoy playful activities. Our healing work provided him with an opportunity to retrieve the innocence and magic of his youth and at the same reset his karmic clock.

So, how does this all apply to resetting our karmic clock? Our spiritual blueprint contains our karmic lesson plan. These lessons include distortions associated with energy patterns of our past and present lifetimes. Remember, these physical, mental and emotional imprints or patterns are artificial programs. When they are removed, they are no longer able to take us out of the present moment and into the false, past experience. As we clear our karmic history, we are able to operate and live from our higher consciousness and tap into our soul wisdom.

The retrieval and subsequent integrating of previously unavailable soul parts allows us to explore our individual consciousness. It is our personal key to unlocking the true nature of the Universe. We all have the ability to be or create anything, *literally.* We have access to the blueprints of all things in creation. This allows us to use the healing essence of other living things, such as herbs, crystals or animals for our healing process. This links us to all of Nature. We are one with *All That Is*.

I have observed that each individual will find their own ways of connecting with their soul. For me it is through meditation and being in nature. For others it may be through a physical means like running, biking or martial arts. Use whatever activity helps achieve alignment, or opens your connection to Source. I found that once I tapped into Source, finding my purpose was easier as well. We can start to explore this by feeling how interlinked we are with nature. A nice place to start is to walk into the woods and sit quietly with a tree. Listen, feel and just be with the tree. That which is in ourselves, is also in the tree and we can link our vibration to the same frequency or atomic level. When we sense our connection to all things, we begin to understand that our actions impact and affect all things.

I have found that a very effective technique for resetting our karmic clock is through service to others. For many of us, being of service *is* our karmic purpose. Discovering how we may best serve others is vital to our survival, happiness and our ability to thrive in this world.

All humanity is in a period of revelation and expansion of consciousness. We are all pioneers in this dimension, uncovering and collecting data for the recovery of our souls. We are also acting on behalf of all beings who are unable to act for themselves or are not in a physical body at this time. We are the explorers of this dimension, and have access to a plethora of information regarding medicine, spirituality and psychology. What we integrate at this time will be the foundation, or template, that individuals and our society will build on for the future. Some of us may arrive sooner than others and hold the door open for those who arrive later. Some will stay in the same old existence on the physical plane, while others will jump up and blaze new paths. As we learn and grow, we bring this expanded energy to our old life situations, such as our work places, families and communities. Old paradigms can be shifted simply by our presence. Our positive energy ripples out and affects those around us. Living in the blessed ordinary can also help others with their gentle evolution.

When we operate from this new space of infinite possibilities, we are in alignment with Source, and everything we need shows up to support us. The Karmic Clock is reset and we are truly in the moment. This is the key to manifesting our life as our authentic selves.

PART THREE

The Way

The Way: *1. A means of entry or exit from somewhere, such as a door or gate. 2. The route, road, street or course of travel. 3. A person's characteristic, method, style, or manner of behavior or expression. 4. A path someone or something would progress in a specified direction, if unobstructed.*

CHAPTER TEN

Uncovering Our Authentic Selves

"Underneath your life experience, beliefs, emotional patterns and cycles of behavior, you are already whole. The part of you that is an aspect of God consciousness is patiently waiting for you to uncover it. Then, life's exploration of your authentic nature can begin."
~Master Saint Germain

Some of us move unconsciously through life, reacting to outside events instead of creating them out of deliberate intent. This absent-minded behavior, driven by old patterns and habits, is a key factor that keeps us from uncovering our authentic selves. When we begin to pay attention and become observers of our own thoughts and behaviors, we have the ability to see how some of them are not serving us anymore.

A computer needs maintenance activities to keep it running at optimal performance, such as de-fragging, eliminating and updating old programs and files and clearing viruses. Similarly, we also need to periodically clear out old mental patterns, toxic thoughts, and memories that are holding us back and no longer serving us. In order for personal growth to occur, we have to let go of old mental programs and discard obsolete beliefs. This can only be uncovered by self-examination.

Establishing a higher level of spiritual awareness allows us to choose the quality of life that we desire. How can we link our consciousness to our every day activities when we are not sure what or where our consciousness is? There is no one-size-fits-all correct answer for everyone.

Our consciousness interacts with our personal experiences to create moment-to-moment revelations for us. At this point it is all about the discovery, not getting all the answers. We can relate this thought to the old adage of 'life is a journey, not a destination,' for it surely fits here.

Our spiritual skills are like tools in our tool belts of life. The most powerful way to use these tools is to link our consciousness with our authentic selves, through *practice, consistency* and *enjoyment*. This means finding the spiritual tools that you enjoy and practicing them on a regular basis. For instance, I meditate every morning and evening at the same time. It has become an important spiritual ritual for me, and something that I do not even need to think about. Spending time in quiet meditation keeps me connected to my authentic self. The fact that I also enjoy it is why I am able to keep doing it with such consistency. As you strive to gain access to your authentic self, it is important that you find activities that you enjoy and practice them consistently.

In the process of uncovering our authentic selves we feel more connected to the surrounding world and begin to get the bigger picture as we surrender into our piece of the collective tapestry of the Universal Soul. This is every soul's path to Source, and it is where we want to return.

The phrase, 'just being' can be described as the state that we exist in consciously at any given moment. This existence includes our thoughts, emotions, and what our bodies are experiencing at that time. For most of mass consciousness, 'just being' refers to the physical state that reacts to external stimuli. They are unaware of their connection to Source. This may be the extent of their experience in this lifetime.

This deeper state of being or awareness has been called many names: *Spirit, essence, true being, soul self, higher self,* and more. I prefer *authentic self* because, to me, it combines all that I have been with who I am now. It is a complete statement. Once we have explored and experienced being in this state of authenticity, we will realize who we are at our core, and it will manifest our desired existence. Just think what it would have been like to sit with Master Buddha or Master Yeshua, without all the baggage or patterns that most humans have. Having achieved an enlightened state here on Earth, their energy was clear and unencumbered. They were channeling all Spirit and in complete connection to their soul at all the times.

Some of us are called to dwell in the best possible existence, otherwise known as the authentic self. Consider this a deeper level of being that offers a more passionate, delicious state of living intentionally. When you live as your authentic self, then you can create the life you desire.

The opposite of the authentic self is the constructed façade, referring to parts of our personalities that may have been created in response to outside influences. Our reaction may have been based solely upon the way misleading, hostile or threatening life events played out for us. If, for example, a child's authentic self expressed creativity at two years of age by drawing on the wall with colorful markers, the child may have been punished. That child may have made a decision, from the perspective of a two year old, that artistic expression is neither safe nor good. Being punished or watching a parent's anger may have shut down that part of the child in order to avoid experiencing punishment again. If this person doesn't work through their karmic lessons from this early childhood experience, a potentially gifted artist may not take the chance to step into their power fully through art, and could end up living a life that is less than fulfilling.

I recently experienced a reconnection to my authentic self when a friend heard me singing to the radio. He complimented my voice and I responded automatically by saying, "Oh no, I can't sing!" He asked why I believed that when it obviously wasn't true. My mind recalled a memory from first grade, when my choir teacher removed me from the Christmas play choir stating that "my talent did not lie in singing." Embarrassed and humiliated in front of my classmates, I avoided singing situations after that. This recent compliment gave me the opportunity to rewrite my beliefs and align them with my current authentic self, which is that I actually do have a talent for singing after all.

Reactionary behaviors become tiny patterns of energy that affect our ability to function and communicate clearly. They can be recorded and filed away in our brains, nervous systems and cells, get stuck in our mental and emotional subtle bodies, and interlace through other energy systems as well. The importance we give to these experiences can alter and trigger an automatic reaction to any situation that feels similar to these early events. A negative childhood experience can include authority figures, family members, peers or any situation that the mind may link to that past experience, whether it is from this life or another. Over time, we create a paradigm of reactionary behavior and/or thought. These decisions, based on fear, can then become repetitive thought patterns or programs playing in our brains, influencing our day-to-day state of being and our future decisions.

Situations that cause trauma and shock can leave imprints or a residual film on our auras and in various energy systems. At the time of the trauma or experience, bits of our soul may become frozen or trapped at the time of the event. Certain parts of us stop growing and get separated from the whole by forming protective coverings that nullify our authentic selves, or buttons that when pressed, pop us right back into a time and space from our past. Again and again, we keep on reliving these events in an effort to make sense of them, and let go of the negative energy around them. In many cases the experience can be revisited energetically, recognized, examined and released so that the information or lesson can be understood and integrated. When we uncover and recognize our triggers and their associated reactionary behaviors, we may find ourselves going back and revisiting the actions we made that were influenced by the original pattern. By shining the light on these experiences, a complete healing is able to take place many times.

Many of us have had life experiences where we were trying to survive situations of abandonment, or were victims of physical or emotional abuse. We may have hundreds or thousands of reactionary beliefs that we created as defense mechanisms and protective walls to frightening or dangerous situations. It is important to understand the purpose behind the making of these survival tools, and realize that in designing these models for living, we were trying to survive and make our lives more bearable. In the process of uncovering our authentic selves, we are then able to honor our abilities to conceive and carry out creative fabrications that may have saved our lives or those we loved. This may be the case even if it meant being devious or dishonorable. Once we recognize these strategies for what they are, and integrate the experiences into our authentic beings, we can allow the healing to begin.

Early childhood reactionary strategies may be factors holding us back from living authentically. They could be blocking that right someone, perfect home, purposeful career, true purpose or service, special events and things that we truly desire. Take a moment to imagine the life you would like to have, or how something in your current life could be different. Feel the space between the two and take a look at the programs, beliefs and mind chatter filling that area of your life between where you are and where you want to be. When we put our attention on these areas, we can recognize, mend or release them so we can restore, improve and recreate them in alignment with our ever-evolving wants, needs and desires.

One day a friend and I were in the Amethyst Healing Center, when I mentioned to her that I thought I was being called to teach. I had literally just said this when someone knocked on the door. When I opened it, a young woman was standing in the rain with a desperate look on her face. The first words out of her mouth were, "My name is Jenny. I must see you...do you have any time to see me? I think that you are supposed to be my teacher." I stepped back and opened the door so that my friend on the couch could see the visitor. She laughed and said, "Wow, your team works really fast!"

Jenny told me that she had been living a lifestyle that did not feel authentic to her. She felt many aspects of her life were in direct opposition to who she thought she really was, including not liking her physical appearance. She had been staying at a local retreat center in an attempt to re-prioritize her life, but she didn't feel safe there, and had left in tears. On her way out of town she stopped at the internet cafe across the street. When she saw the sign for Amethyst Healing Center, saw my picture and read my brochure, she felt drawn to see me.

Within a month of working together, Jenny had made a profound life shift. Starting with her physical self, she decided that she wanted the outside of her body to reflect who she was on the inside. She had her breast implants removed and some of her tattoos altered or removed. She reviewed every aspect of her life and made radical changes. She is now a jewelry designer, artist, grows and prepares raw organic foods and has learned to do massage. She says she is happy and feels she is living an authentic life. I see her as a prime example of someone who achieved the rewards that are the results of listening to the desires of her soul.

Sometimes, the darkest hours of our lives can be the most opportune times to start the journey of finding our authenticity. Great loss, change, and the stripping away of our comfortable illusions can bring us to the point of a raw and exposed being. *This* is the new beginning. What we perceive as crisis is often the Universe's greatest show of love for us. When we reach the point of feeling that we are in total darkness, we appreciate even the tiniest flickers of light. This process has a special place in my own heart and soul quest.

There was a time I refer to as my thirteen months of shadows. I lost both my parents, valued relationships changed, some even completely left my life, including a relationship with a man I thought I was going to marry. Everything that I believed reflected or confirmed who and what I was had been drastically altered. I saw nothing positive or helpful remaining in my world. All I had left was the elusive Mr. R., my abilities as a massage therapist, and a healing 'gift' that I was uncertain about. I kept this gift a secret because I felt that if I fully revealed it to the wrong people, I could be in danger. I felt fear at a cellular level and knew it came from past-life karmic experiences where I had been killed for my healing abilities. The only comfort and affinity I felt was with my Spirit Guides and Angels, even though I did not fully understand them at the time. Isolated and feeling alone, I began to wish that I could join these angelic beings and reunite with the solace I felt with them.

One night, I desperately needed a good night's sleep and wanted to silence the negative voices in my head. With a heavy heart, I opened a bottle of wine and climbed into the hot tub to relax. The next thing I remember is when I woke up choking on spa water.

As I assessed the situation and realized I had fallen asleep in the hot tub, my mind went into 'what if?' mode. I thought, "What if I didn't wake up and just went home to join the bodiless beings that were a part of my spirit world?" In a strangely detached manner, I explored that possibility. A series of images flashed through my mind, including what my body would look like after floating in the tub. I considered the real possibility that no one would find me for quite some time. My final thought was "What would happen to my dog?"

The loss of all things that represented who I thought I was put me in a position of considering my options. I like to think of this not as the traditional breakdown but as a *breakthrough*, and my soul made a decision. It was from this perspective that I decided to stay in my physical body and commit to uncovering my authentic self. I could only hope to survive and thrive if I became who I was intended to be. My past roles and responsibilities were no longer significant. I would no longer wear the mom, daughter, wife, girlfriend, sister, friend or employee hats. The old, familiar faces were gone and I could not determine who I was by seeing my reflection in their eyes. It was a time of rebirth. I believe I am not alone in my experience, and that others may also have had similar experiences that helped them make important choices that would support them in their decisions to uncover their authentic selves.

As a result of my soulful choice, my intuitive abilities expanded to a higher level. My commitment to life in the physical form gave my Guides the signal they needed to proceed with their plans for me. On the tangible level, it manifested in my selling many of my possessions, changing the way I dressed, leaving my job, and presenting the outside of my body in a manner more consistent with who I was.

Shortly after this experience, I had a vision for a healing center I founded. I had met a friend for lunch in a quaint village about forty miles from where I lived. We were sitting in a restaurant, talking and relaxing, when I glanced across the street and saw a neglected store-front building with weeds growing in front of it. Instantly, an entirely different picture popped into view. I saw the structure lovingly remodeled, complete with a sign for my healing center. You must understand, I had no prior thoughts of moving to or living in this place!

I told my friend that I had to go look at the building. She was surprised and kept asking why I would want that old, vacant and unkempt place. I knew I was guided by Divine Spirit and that I had to act upon this faith. By the end of the day, I had contacted the real estate company that was handling the property and I drove home with a signed lease in my possession.

For three months I planted a garden in the backyard, built walls, figured out what metaphysical products I wanted to sell, and made decisions about many details. People would stop by to ask what kind of business was opening up. I simply stated that it was a healing place. Their question was frequently, "What do you do here?" My automatic response was, "Well, what do you need?" Somehow, it seemed that whatever their request was, I happened to have what they wanted. From healing massage to lavender oil to energy work, they got what they came for and I found myself watching the magic of my fully-aligned authentic self evolve and grow.

I was able to recognize and appreciate the gifts that arrived later on. I would show up in the morning to unlock the door and find that people had left plants, shovels and other additions on the front door step. My garden received a tree, flower cuttings, and even a Goddess statue complete with a fountain. I envisioned garden fairies who must have bestowed these gifts, and my appreciation blossomed.

This experience and many others, are examples of why I am comfortable knowing that my job is to just show up, do what I am guided to do, and trust that the people, places and things I need will rise up to support me. I had a few moments of asking 'How will I do this?' The biggest source of my anxiety was truly embracing who I was in a public scope. I could no longer stay 'under the radar' which had been one of my comfort-driven beliefs, or assume that the right people would find me by word of mouth. My decision to open a healing center moved me out of my comfort zone and, not without accident, led me to fully actualize the life I desired.

I realize that I had a bit of help staying on track and focusing on my goals. Becoming truly authentic would have been a more difficult process without the aid of my Spirit Guides, Angels and Ascended Master Teachers who told me that my value to those around me hinges on my personal alignment with Source.

CHAPTER ELEVEN

Spirit Guides, Angels & Ascended Master Teachers

"Your Spirit Guides, Angels and Ascended Master Teachers are your Divine Team. Their purpose is to help you utilize their gifts. In assisting you, they can fulfill their soul's Dharma."
~Archangel Zadkiel

Ascend: Go up or climb. Rise through the air. Rise in pitch. A spiritual being or soul that has risen into heaven.

Master: A skilled practitioner of a particular art or activity. Title and set expression. Acquired knowledge, skill, technique and accomplishment. Able to teach others with proficiency.

Ascended Master: Spiritually-enlightened, fifth-dimensional beings, who in past incarnations were ordinary humans in physical bodies. They have undergone a series of spiritual transformations, and acquired the wisdom and mastery needed to become immortal and free of the cycles of re-embodiment and karma. These beings have been given the title Ascended Master Teacher.

If you have chosen to read this book, you have probably felt the presence of your Spirit Guides and Angels at one time or another. Some people speak to and hear them as I do. Children are very aware of their spirit helpers, since they have not learned to fear what they see or hear. They may think of them as their invisible friends. As adults, I have noticed people have a tendency to first see Angels or Spirit Guides they believe to be Angels. I think this is because in our society Angels are a safer image to consider.

As humans, we struggle with the concept of unconditional love. Dealing with our karma and life difficulties means we are rarely there for each other in this way, or even understand what it means. Our Spirit Guides, Angels and Ascended Master Teachers are aware of the stream of love, guidance, and support we receive from Source, and see that we may not be able to receive this flow directly from Spirit ourselves. We may feel more comfortable accessing segmented, limited versions of Source energy. They can bridge the gap for us and are our connection to Source in a way that is safe and not overwhelming.

Spirit Guides and Angels show themselves to us in many forms, depending on our path, perception and purpose at the time. They may come to us as animals, tree spirits, Devas, spirits of a place, or as ancestors or beings from past lives. They can come to us as voices, in the form of light or as a feeling that someone is present with us. These are the beings that hear us when we pray or meditate and are with us throughout our lives.

Those of us who are healers or light workers in some way may also have a living Master Teacher or Ascended Master Teachers who guide us in our work. Spirit Guides, Angels and Ascended Master Teachers are souls who walked the human path filled with obstacles and challenges, and have returned as spirit allies. All of them are beings who work directly with Divine Source and with each other to assist with mass awakening and unfolding of humanity. Their intention has always been to support humans on their path to enlightenment. They too evolve on their path to full re-unification with Source. It is as if we are down here in the trenches, so to speak, and our Team, as I refer to them, are sending us supplies and information needed for us to win our karmic battles in our human forms.

A Spirit Guide I referred to as Mr. R. first appeared to me as a pirate-looking male presence that felt like a kindly uncle energy. I now know that he has been with me since childhood. I recognize his energy as the invisible friend my grandmother told me about, and who I relied upon as a child to always be there. He comforted me and his voice became the voice of reason in my head. Later, he showed up in purple flames and would assist me while I massaged clients. I would see my clients skin glow purple under my touch. After I opened my Amethyst Healing Center, I finally learned his name and that others worked with him, too.

In my second month of business, a woman came in to Amethyst Healing Center. She was on vacation, one of many tourists who pass through our village, and wanted a massage. About halfway through her session, as I asked her to turn over and lay on her back, she began to look around the room. Usually, when someone receives a massage, they close their eyes and focus on the relaxing touch. However, this lady was obviously concerned about the space she was in and finally asked, "Who are you working with, in here?" Thinking she meant the other people who were in the building or were part of the healing collective, I started to describe them. She stopped me, "No, no, I mean who is in *this* room, working with *you*?" She gestured toward the spot in the room where Mr. R., my personal Spirit Guide, always positioned himself. I hesitated and cautiously asked, "Can you see him?"

She then proceeded to identify him as Master Saint Germain. My first thought, which I lost no time telling her, was "He's no

Saint and he isn't a Master." To me, he was just my purple clad, pirate-looking, visible to only me, Spirit Guide. How dare she try to tell me who he was? To make matters worse, she started to explain that he was an Ascended Master who worked with healers all over the world. I was indignant and shook my head no! However, as I was denying what she was telling me, I looked over at Mr. R., and he was nodding his head in affirmation, meaning that what she said was true. I felt betrayed. Here I was, running my own healing center and I had to find out who my Spirit Guide was from a stranger!

After she left, my hurt and sense of betrayal remained. He had been a solid support to me for the last six years and had cradled me in his arms through my darkest times. I felt he had kept secrets from me and my ego was bruised considerably. I refused to talk with Mr. R. and decided to ignore him.

But Mr. R., or Master Saint Germain, whoever he was, was not going to let me go easily. He began to communicate with me in new ways, such as having a specific book fall off my library shelf and open to a page about a Master Rakoczi, a Hungarian nobleman. To my surprise, he was connected to Master Saint Germain. As my mind opened and his presence expanded, I began to realize that he had been an influence throughout my entire life and finally, he had presented himself in a manner that had been very easy for me to accept. I believe that if I had known who he was sooner, I might not have had as pure a relationship with him. My perception of him would have been skewed under another's perception of who he was. If he had appeared to me first as a Master, I might have rebelled or been frightened. Instead, my pirate friend, who told me to call him Mr. R. (not Master), endeared himself to me. Eventually we resumed our partnership, and with this new knowledge I found my capabilities as a healer advancing. I soon learned about several other Ascended Masters.

I have access to at least twenty-seven Spirit Guides, Angels and Ascended Master Teachers that I now work with. Some introduced themselves to me directly, some were introduced through Master Saint Germain, and at times I have called a couple of them in for help. Depending upon the circumstances of my clients and their Spirit Guides, the actual number varies. I have learned that if a person finds their way to me, it is often due to the prompting of Spirit Guides that we share.

These Divine beings are as real to me as other humans. My relationships with them have developed through years of meditation and healing work. Here is a current list of *My Team* in alphabetical order with a brief description of each:

Master Buddha: To me, he represents laughter, bliss and gratitude for the blessed ordinary. He assists me in meditation, clearing my energy and joyfully quieting my mind. Like Jesus, he attained enlightenment while in physical form. To me, Master Jesus and Master Buddha share the same Christly energy.

Master Commander Ashtar & The Galactic Command: They are fifth dimensional extraterrestrial beings. They assist us with the electromagnetic field of the Earth, ley lines, faults, volcanoes, vortexes, and other power energy transmitters. I assist Commander Ashtar in inter-dimensional planetary clearing, and anything that may need a witness's testimony or focused attention from a human perspective. Master Commander Ashtar usually comes to me, without words, dressed in a silver uniform as a summons to be an advocate for the Earth and humankind.

Master Djwhal Khul: He showed up while I was working with a client who needed spiritual surgery, and has stayed working with me ever since. He facilitates in the capacity of a spiritual surgeon. He uses his energy with a laser precision ability to clear and balance on many levels. He is always at my left, and has become an integral member of *My Team*.

Master El Morya: To me, he is the strong, silent one. He is the teacher of several Masters I work with. At first I had difficulties being fully present at his higher frequency, and when attempting to channel him, I would fall unconscious. Now I am able to intuit his information easily.

Master Hilarian: He helps with the retrieval of soul pieces and clears debris from the energy systems so that the returning soul part can be reintegrated.

Master Kathumi: He came on the scene while I was working with a client, and is now a regular member of *My Team*. He is a Teacher of Teachers, and has been known to appear on the physical plane. He helps me to access the Akashic Record Library, conducts past life research, and facilitates soul retrieval.

Master Kuan Yin: She is the Goddess of compassion and protection particularly for women and children. I have seen her step forward when I work with women who have been victims of tyranny or abuse. As the female incarnation of the Buddha consciousness, she carries Divine Mother and Divine Feminine energies. Feminine warrior energy is her forte.

Master Maha Chohan: He carries massive Christly energy. During a meditation, he showed me my connection to all things in the big picture by wrapping his energy around me, lifting me out of my body and taking me up to view my world from far above. I was able to comprehend just a fraction of how my physical and spiritual bodies were joined with everything all the way to a galactic level.

Master Mary Magdalene: She represents the Divine Feminine and holds the keys to sacred sexuality for the female. She is wife, sister, mother, lover and female friendship. I ask for her help when I'm working with male clients who are in troubled relationships with women or if I am involved in a relationship with a man myself. She is Master Yeshua's Divine counterpart and companion.

Master Melchezadek: He shares with me the sacred geometric symbols or keys that open doors to higher planes of awareness. He also assists me with integration of the higher frequencies and templates for manifesting new plans.

Master Mother Mary: For me she represents the Divine Mother. Her energy is loving and compassionate. I call on her when I, my students or clients need unconditional mothering or nurturing energy. She is great when I work with children, animals or even when I am making a big pot of something yummy on the stove. She adds her love to it.

Master Saint Francis: He introduced himself to me just before I left for my planetary healing trip in Italy. He works with animals and children, and has a wonderful connection to Mary Magdalene. He was my host in Italy, assisting me with my planetary healing assignment there. He led me to lesser known power spots where I could perform my work undisturbed.

Master Saint Germain/Mr. R.: This is the first Spirit Guide I was aware of and he has been with me as long as I can remember. He came to me looking like a pirate, with the jovial quality of a dear uncle. He is playful, bold and a jokester. He shows up in purple light that moves like fire, known as the *Violet Flame*. The Violet Flame is the highest frequency in the visible spectrum and it transforms energy at an atomic level. It was and still is used by alchemists of the Spirit. Master Saint Germain's alchemical nature helps me in my healing work by combining, transmuting and transforming energy to a higher frequency. He guided me in naming and opening the Amethyst Healing Center. He was, and still is, my constant companion and the gatekeeper or host to all other energetic beings that appear.

Master Serapis Bey: He acts as the ambassador and translator for me with connecting to beings from other dimensions, worlds and alien species. I ask for his help when clients, whose past lives have been in non-human incarnations, are having challenges adapting to the human body.

Master Yeshua/Jesus/The Christ: His name means: *To deliver, save or rescue.* He came to me as Yeshua in the beginning. My religious background would have blocked me from accepting him as Jesus or Christ. I believe The Christ energy existed before Jesus of Nazareth was born. Yeshua carries the Divine Masculine and when called into the circle, I get the physical sensation of being blown back to the point of feeling my hair move. He is so powerful, loving and almost overwhelming. I have called on him for help with life-threatening illnesses, and for protection when working with dark energy. He oversees the work of the Ascended Masters as a whole.

> ***Angels:*** *Angels are supernatural beings or spirits, often depicted in humanoid form with feathered wings on their backs and halos around their heads. They are mostly androgynous, but some do have male or female characteristics. Angels are Divine messengers of Source, delivering prayers and messages to humans asking for help through prayer. Angels are attendants or agents for humanity and are intermediaries between Source and Earth, as guardians, spirits or a guiding influence protecting and carrying out tasks for Source.*
>
> ***Archangels:*** *Archangels are chief, high ranking, or leading Angels. The three most well known Archangels are Michael, Gabriel and Raphael. There are many philosophies on the actual number of Archangels. These are the ones I work with.*

Archangel Amethyst: She showed up first in the garden just before I opened Amethyst Healing Center. She holds the focus of light and the violet flame there and is the reason the center stays energetically clean. I did not realize her name was genuine until someone brought in a picture of her, six months later, with Zadkiel, Saint Germain and Lady Portia. I thought that Amethyst was a name I had assigned her. Who would have thought? Confirmation!

Archangel Ariel: Meaning: *Lion of God*. She assists with information retrieval and healing. She carries messages, prayers and aids with sending healing energies over long distances.

Archangel Azreal: Meaning: *Whom God helps*. He came into the room while I was working with a client and pops in from time to time. He specifically helps me work with young men who are troubled or who have a history with drug abuse. He also assists the souls of people who are crossing over.

Archangel Chamuel: Meaning: *He who sees God*. Works with clients dealing with heartbreak, issue with love and relationship dynamics.

Archangel Gabriel: Meaning: *Strength of God*, As the music keeper he sends me information through music. Have you ever awoken with a song in your head and it is just what you needed to know for some event that took place during your day? This is an example of how he works with me.

Archangel Haniel: Meaning: *The grace of God*. She came to me while I was working with a client and stayed on as part of My Team. She shows us the pleasures in life and helps us see the beauty of the planet.

Archangel Jophiel: Meaning: *Beauty of God*. He is playful, loves art and he helps us open up to our creative sides.

Archangel Metatron: Meaning: *Keeper of the watch*. Metatron is very powerful and works with sacred geometry. He is a record keeper and at times assists Master Melchezadeck and Archangel Michael. Often, Angels appear androgynous to me, however Metatron looks more masculine when I see him. He is also said to have been Enoch from the Old Testament, one of the only humans to become an angelic being.

Archangel Michael: Meaning: *He who is like God*. He is one of the most powerful Archangels and is the one who disposes or recycles negative energies. I call on him for protection, for he is a guardian of the planet. He gives me assistance when I have an especially large or nasty job to do. He assists me in understanding, locating and transcending darkness. Master Saint Germain introduced me to Archangel Michael, early on, in my work. Subsequently, Michael brought the other Archangels through to me.

Archangel Raphael: Meaning: *God heals*. Raphael is all about healing and the heart chakra and uses an amazing green energy. He assists me in every healing I do. He also bridges the expanse when I am involved in long distance healing.

Archangel Uriel: Meaning: *Fire of God*. He assists with the retrieval of past life information and contracts. He lights the way when I need to travel through the astral plain or to different dimensions and brings me home safely.

Archangel Zadkiel: Meaning: *Righteousness of God*. Due to his close contact with Master Saint Germain, I realized that he as been with me since I was a child. He assists Master Saint Germain as the bearer of the violet flame. He also works closely with Archangel Michael and is a travel companion for me through the astral and dimensional plains.

As my abilities and skills as a clairvoyant developed, I became adept at recognizing other people's Spirit Guides and Angels. It expanded to my becoming a go-between for my clients, interpreting and communicating to them what their Spirit Guides were here to assist them with.

My first occasion dealing with someone else's Spirit Guide was my oldest son Trenton's 'friend,' named Jarred, who was invisible to all but him.

I came home from work one night, ready to watch some TV. As I settled in, I heard a sound as though the front door opened. Knowing that it was locked and I was not expecting anyone, I got up to see what I had heard. Walking down the hallway, the bathroom nightlight shed enough light for me to see that no one was there. As I stood there, I caught movement out of the corner of my eye in Trenton's bedroom. Peering into his room in the dim light, I could see that his ceiling fan was on, and that several books and small toys were circling the blades as if they were flying. Not wanting to take my eyes off the scene before me, I groped on the wall for the light switch. I turned it on and watched in amazement as the items all fell to the floor. I looked over at Trenton's bed and saw him sitting up, looking at me.

I asked him, "Are you okay?" He said, "Yes." Not sure if he was afraid, I asked him if he wanted to sleep in my room. His reply was, "No, it's okay."

I tucked him back in, turned off the light and went to bed. We did not discuss the incident right away. I believe that we mentally shelved it until we could process it. Several weeks later, when we were on a trip in the car, I brought it up. Trenton looked at me with exasperation and said, "Mom, I told you it's Jarred that does all of that stuff."

Although Trenton had been telling me about Jarred since he was four years old, I finally had some proof that he might be telling the truth, and decided to research the information Jarred had given Trenton. With my limited experience at the time, I had decided that my son had an undesirable spirit attachment or was being haunted. I made plans to conduct a séance, which we did at Trenton's thirteenth birthday party, with the help of his friends. I felt it was my job to 'send Jarred into the light.' To kick him out, in other words. But during the séance, Jarred revealed himself as Trenton's Spirit Guide, and made it clear he was not going anywhere!

Once I accepted Jarred as part of our family, I had to set some ground rules with this mischievous spirit being who was wreaking havoc with the order of my home. Jarred agreed to stop messing with the electronics and moving household items around. I consented not to try to send him away, and would not interfere with his assignment with Trenton. It ended up being a workable situation.

We humans are the present assignment of our Spirit Guides, Angels and Ascended Master Teachers. Some come and go during different parts of our life, depending on our needs. I found that when I started working with my Spirit Guides and asked them to blend their soul essence with mine, I became better at identifying them. They each have a different feel, color, smell, sound or physical object that represents them. For instance, Master Saint Germain shows up in purple, has a feisty, playful feel, and his symbol to me is the fleur-de-lis. Master Djwhal Khul shows up in turquoise, is very serious and his symbol to me is the dragonfly. By blending their energy with mine, they have helped me with my own healing, healing for others, given me clarity on issues, or just shared information I needed to know.

I remember so many experiences with these helpmates, even silly little situations. The Angels, specifically, were insistent that I use them for help with shopping, food selection and even getting parking places. Yes, there really are parking Angels. I was instructed to call upon them, no matter how trivial it might seem. In the beginning, I was always questioning my abilities, their existence and asking for proof. You know… "If you are real, then show me a fool-proof sign, something that without a doubt can only be from you."

There was the time I really wanted purple flannel sheets for my bed. At the time flannel sheets came pretty much in standard plaid, forest green or off-white. Purple was not a popular color back then. So I asked for my sheets in a very specific manner. I entered the department store with a doubtful mind, totally expecting to be leaving without my purple sheets. To my surprise, I turned down the sheet aisle and sitting right at the front of the shelf was a set of dark purple, flannel sheets in the right size. The cost was reasonable and I remember holding the package next to my body and not believing it was real. I actually had to sit down and get my bearings back as I was in a bit of shock. I still have those sheets. They are not as fuzzy as they used to be but I love them because they were my first bit of proof amongst many doubts that *My Team* is real. It may sound silly, but it was confirming. This was a starting point, and after that the signs they sent me became more powerful and meaningful. This was the beginning of trusting the information I received from *My Team*.

My own experience with recognizing and giving names and identities to my Spirit Guides has been varied. Archangel Michael introduced himself, and was quite forthcoming with his purpose on my path. Master Mary Magdalene's presence came to me as I was helping male clients with issues in their primary female relationships. She taught me how to use the Divine Feminine energy to create safe and healthy boundaries with men. Master Buddha, who first appeared as nothing more than a big, jolly, loving energy, has been with me since I started meditating. He also showed me how to protect and cleanse my personal energy while doing healing work.

Getting to know your personal Spirit Guides is an ongoing lifelong exploration, so play with it and have fun. They will never infringe on your free will. We are free to choose how we would like to live in this lifetime, but they may make suggestions and guide us in certain directions. Mine enjoy a dark chocolate and good coffee now and then. I really believe I provide sensual memories for them to enjoy.

If you are interested in meeting your Spirit Guides and Angels, you can start by choosing one or two you recognize and feel most comfortable with. For example, Christians throughout the world have a deep relationship with Master Jesus The Christ and Master Mother Mary. Or perhaps, the energy of Master Buddha or Master Kuan Yin may feel safer. These teachers who once had human forms and walked the Earth remain close to the planet to help all of us with our spiritual unfolding.

CHAPTER TWELVE

The Way Seers

"Psychic abilities are a gift from God and natural to every being on Earth. Remember, it is only through your Divine heart that you can see things as they truly are."
~Master Mother Mary

Way Seer: *Way seers are psychics, clairvoyants and light workers. They are the mystic carriers of the flame and seers of the way. They light our way and inspire others with their passion, keeping us on the path that our souls have laid out for us.*

Spiritual Teachers, Hindu Gurus, Zen Buddhists, Tibetan Monks, Shamanic Elders, and Ascended Master Teachers all recommend that we not dwell on or get sidetracked with our psychic abilities at any stage of our spiritual development. As we become more aware, practice different healing techniques, including meditation, we are bound to open up to our connection to Source. It is not wise to get stuck in the excitement and glamour that heightened psychic awareness may sometimes bring. What is most important is that we get to the principal beneficial practices and disciplines of the mind. This is especially true if we have been a victim of abuse, come from a culture or background where we worked mostly with our brain, on the physical plane, or have more personal healing to do before we work on behalf of others. I do not believe it is possible to attain any sort of spiritual enlightenment without psychic awareness. The two go hand in hand and expand at an equivalent rate.

There are certain qualities that one must acquire before they can fully actualize their psychic abilities. These include being of service to others and the planet, quieting the mind chatter to create internal peace, having clear energy systems, a firm connection to Soul and Source, mastery of the senses, possessing compassion, humility, integrity, and being free of attachments. Before we draw on our psychic gifts, it is important for us to attain these qualities, have genuine purpose and approach the world with an open heart.

Manifesting psychic abilities is thought to have detrimental effects on one's spiritual development until we have had what I like to call *the glimpsing*. I am referring to that moment when we get a glimpse of what it is like to be one with All. It is also called *Buddha-mind*. When we get to the place where we experience ourselves as one with the Universe, we can then appreciate all things, and our psychic capacities blossom. Once we achieve it, then can we begin to understand our purpose and what kind of responsibility the gift may carry.

I believe that every one of us has the tools to pick up the energies and frequencies of the planet and everything in it. It is a matter of developing our muscles, so to speak. Everyone has their own way of receiving or sending psychic information. The Masters strongly recommend that before we engage our talents in this area we develop the above listed characteristics as well as personal clarity, healthy emotional boundaries, and a surrendered ego, which I define as the ability to follow Divine guidance. These senses have more meaning to us than psychic pictures, feelings or words we do not understand or comprehend. It is really about how whole, healed, honest and free of baggage we are, so that we are able to show up, get out of the way and be a clean clear channel for Source.

To promote understanding, let us look at what avenues these abilities may take. The following are definitions of how our senses are enhanced by our psychic abilities and all forms of extra-sensory perception.

Clairaudience: To perceive extra sensory sounds or noise broadcasted from the spiritual or ethereal realm, in the form of 'inner ear' or mental tones which are perceived without the aid of the physical ear and beyond the limitations of ordinary time and space.

Claircognizance: A person acquires psychic knowledge about others primarily by means of intrinsic knowledge. It is the ability to know something without a physical explanation of why you know it.

Clairgustance: The paranormal ability that allows one to perceive the essence or taste of a substance from the ethereal or spiritual realm without putting anything in one's mouth.

Clairessence: Wherein a person accesses psychic knowledge through the physical sense of smell. For example, I smell lilacs every time my grandmother visits me in spirit form. When I smell lilacs during a session, it is my signal that the grandmother of the person I am reading for has joined us.

Clairsentience: To feel the vibration of other people, plants, animals, places and things. There are many different degrees of clairsentience, ranging from the thoughts or emotions of others to the perception of diseases.

Clairvoyance: A clairvoyant is one who receives extrasensory impressions and symbols in the form of 'inner sight,' or mental images, which are perceived without the aid of the physical eyes and beyond the limitations of ordinary time and space.

These different avenues of psychic ability become stronger and more accurate when we come from a place of understanding and love. We then are able to see, speak, taste, hear and sense for ourselves and others what is true.

> **Truth:** *1. The quality or state of being true. 2. That which is true or in accordance with fact or reality. 3. A fact or belief that is accepted as true.*

I find the definition of 'accepted as true' interesting. It is having an agreement with a group or mass consciousness that this is our truth about this matter. As the paradigm shifts, so do our perceptions of what is true and we find ourselves dropping out of agreements of our past to hold true to our new beliefs.

I have many clients come to me because they are not sure if they are being lied to. This is because they have not developed internal discernment skills. It is amazing how many of us have no idea how to recognize truth or detect untruths. This may be due to parental, religious or social programming. All of us have been lied to, which leads us to lie to others, and even to ourselves. In our society it is actually okay not to tell the truth or to exaggerate or embellish it. Our minds have manufactured thought patterns to close ourselves off from the truth as if we are pulling a blind over our own eyes. Our willingness to lie to ourselves keeps us stuck in repetitive thinking. All the patterns and false beliefs we are still carrying around are actually keeping us from sensing truth in all things.

Integrity, morals and honesty are all intriguing ideas in the world at this time. The planet is so impacted with dishonesty that there are even degrees of deceit classified by using phrases like 'little white lie' or the catch-all term, 'gray area.' In this environment, we often do not have the ability to discern the truth from a lie. We are raised hearing parents, teachers and community leaders use the phrase 'it was for your own good' as justification for not telling us everything and essentially being deceptive.

When he was four years old, my oldest son Trenton came home one day from school and was very upset. He asked me if it was true that there was no Santa Claus. Was it really his father and I who put the gifts under the tree after he went to sleep on Christmas Eve? At this point I tried to rationalize to him that Saint Nicholas was a real person and that we keep his spirit alive by giving gifts. And then I tried to explain the Jesus story to him. But, all he could say is, "You mean every mom and dad all over the world *lies* to their kids? Even the TV lies? Santa is DEAD?" Yep, here it comes… "So, does that mean there isn't an Easter Bunny or Tooth Fairy either?" I watched as Trenton's childhood belief system took a hit and crashed. As he tried to put all the pieces of his world back together from this new truth, he had trouble trusting me. This experience really caused me to re-think the whole idea about making up untrue or misleading stories for our children, believing it causes no harm. It is no wonder, as a culture, we have trouble recognizing truth when we have been lied to by our parents, teachers and trusted advisors, the very people who we trust most in the world.

Prior to safely experimenting with our psychic potential it is essential to have a sense of truth, recognizing it and speaking it. Knowing the difference between the truth and a lie is critical when working with and traveling through the etheric realm, dealing with negative energies, and undesirable or devious spirits. Standing in truth can keep us on track so that we only get the highest truth possible, the true images and symbols that we are looking for. Many lower frequency psychics, fake prophets, and so-called fortune-tellers are not accurate at being able to tell the truth from something false. It is crucial to run anything others say to us through our own individual truth-meter.

Being able to recognize the truth is vital because there are many planes of existence that carry a magnitude of information. Some of these planes of existence are sourced from Spirit, others are powered by the spirit of a lower frequency or are thought forms created by people or mass consciousness emotions. These lower energies or creations made by the collective are being birthed by everyone's beliefs all day long, every day.

In the beginning of my channeling and intuiting process, there were instances when I added my personal perspective to the Masters' messages. What happened was that the information stopped flowing until I backed up and rephrased the meaning to represent only what they had said. Immediately, the connection resumed. In that manner, I was shown Truth as the Masters saw it and needed to have it told. I learned to step aside and allow the true information to come through me instead of from me. It was a valuable lesson.

In the layering or pages of records in the Akashic library, information can appear different to every reader. There is a recording of illusions, or glamour, that comes from our mental and emotional patterns and beliefs. They are the un-truths of our history and that of an area, person, or thing and are often fueled by mass consciousness thoughts and feelings. These can be accessed through the fourth dimension or astral plane. This is where hit-and-miss psychics and fortune-tellers read from or tap into. This is not the space that I or anyone would be interested in receiving information from, due to the smoke and mirror effect it projects. Giving someone this information may strengthen their illusions and keep them stuck. I compare it to looking through a person's trash to give them information about themselves, when really what is needed is the truth from a higher perspective. None of us would want just anyone poking around in our records that could not tell the truth from a lie.

The energy of an event leaves an impression on us, in time, on things and on areas of land. Places on the planet have Akashic records just like people do. It is here that all the events that took place in or around an area are recorded. With help from our Spirit Guides we can gain access to these records and be privy to all the layering of information about any given place, thing, event or person, with permission.

The land, stones and bodies of water carry the energy of the history of a place. We can sit on a rock or bathe in a pond and connect with the energy of the surroundings. We can feel, see, know or sense the layering of events from the past. Some of the energies that are left behind may not, in fact, be accurate about the area or people that have been there before. If we came along and leaned against a tree where someone may have sat, fantasizing or dreaming about something that never took place, would we be able to read the imprinted energy of the tree correctly? Could we tell the difference between the fantasy and what actually occurred? There may be a chance that one may report something that never took place, if they were not able to tell them apart.

Healing our past is a critical part of this process. Unless we heal our pasts, we might have a tendency to do to others what was done to us, without even being aware of it. We make unconscious choices out of habit, attracting the same situations over and over, creating cycles of behavior. It is important to realize that we are not stuck in these holding patterns. When we become consciously aware of a pattern, and shed light on it, then we can make a conscious choice to heal and clear the pattern. Evolved cognitive thinking, derived from our heart, grounded in our physical body, with the ability to connect to Source, will take us out of despair. True healing is possible when we choose to do the work and reclaim our power of conscious choice. Only then will we be able to see the truth.

When we draw on our psychic abilities it is essential that we do so with an open heart filled with compassion, love and empathy. If the heart is congested with envy, judgment and hate, we cannot know love or truth. We require space in our heart to allow love from Source to flow through, filling our lives, and touching those around us. Truth is recognized in the heart and can create an opening for healing. An open heart and a connection to Spirit is more powerful than any psychic ability. It is our key to discerning our way through life.

Psychic abilities are natural to all of us. For example, if you start to leave a restaurant late at night to walk to your car alone and you feel the hair on the back of your neck stand up like someone is watching you, you may make the last minute decision to wait inside and walk out with a friend. That extrasensory perception may have saved your life.

When our chakras are clear and open, we are able to channel our soul and Source frequencies freely. When our soul connection is developed and is more present in our day-to-day life than that of our old patterns, we move from having a psychic connection to having a spiritual connection. Being psychic starts by having clarity on the third and fourth dimensions, and when our chakras are able to perceive sound and light using the mental body to translate. *Spirituality* means having clarity on all dimensions and transmitting information through all of the energy systems. Plainly, a higher frequency of awareness is essential when deciding the right use of information we receive.

When I hear truth, I get goose bumps just above my knees. This is clairsentience. It is the ability to feel the energy in our body as it moves through us. This energy gets processed in the third and fourth chakras. It also alerts our brain, like a hunch, about something or the answer to a complicated question that just popped into our mind. It is the fuel for our 'A-ha' moments.

We can discern the difference in the energy between our

Spirit Guides, Angels and Ascended Master Teachers from a lower level of energy that carries fear or anger. Their energy will always be filled with the unconditional love of Spirit. Our hearts will pick up on this immediately. Even if their message is fierce, it will be delivered with love. The higher our frequency is, the higher the frequency we will be able to receive from them.

If you decide to give an energy or psychic reading to another person, as you relay information that you receive, pay attention to how the energy feels in *your* chakras, which will help you determine if you are interpreting it correctly. It ought to feel as if a key is opening the multi-faceted constructs of their energy fields, and in this way you can get the next piece of the story. Be careful not to predict an outcome, which may be a sign that you are adding your own energy to the mix. We are only taking an evaluation of the moment and energies surrounding the issue. That person could leave the room and change his or her mind, due to their free will, and the entire outcome could change.

Highly sensitive people may have feelings of impending danger or massive change when something is about to happen that mass consciousness is destined to experience. These incidents include a natural disaster or a global experience that we are experiencing collectively, that can not in any way be altered or prevented by our participation. Our future can often be changed by altering our beliefs and actions. When viewing the future, be careful not to make predictive statements.

To share in the receiving of another's deepest thoughts, private feelings and personal history is an honor, and can impact us at a very raw human level. Connecting empathically to someone in this way is a gift. Allow the person you are working with to explain to you what it means to them. In this way they can do their own work while you observe and create a safe space for their unfolding. Do not cloud their experiences with your ideas or encourage them to become dependent on you. Empower those we read for to learn to do this themselves, and they will be more apt to gain strength and confidence in their own ability to heal. Just being understood can be a most validating and affirming experience for anyone.

The ***Clairaudient Chakras*** are located just above the ears. Although they have not been listed in the top, or most popular of the chakras, they have a very major role in the chakra system. The energy flows to us on waves of sound frequencies that feel like they are being heard inside our heads. These waves of energy can come in the form of mind chatter from those around you, voices, music and tones. When our Spirit Guides, Angels and Ascended Master Teachers speak to us, it is in a high frequency filled with truth or divinity that can be felt in our energy systems and body, perhaps in the form of goose bumps or just a sense of knowing. Their information will be filled with love, have relevance and be precisely what you need to hear.

We can be fooled by clairaudient transmissions by lower consciousnesses. Some spirits of a lesser frequency may want to contact you if they see you as 'shiny' or sensitive. Usually they just want attention by giving you information or concepts that are not clear or have little worth. Check your heart and gut reaction before accepting what is being conveyed. When the sender is legitimate, the information will be of service to the receiver in some way and will not have its own agenda. Lesser energies will not be able to connect you with Divine knowledge, incite wisdom or open doors to your personal learning.

Our chakras receive and perceive the world around us in a unique way. For those of you who are way seers, let's delve deeper into the chakra system and see how to interpret messages through these channels from a clairsentient perspective.

The first or root chakra takes in information about our surroundings and assigns it a worth, sending a message to our brains. If it senses danger, the message is marked red, saying

"Emergency!" When reading the energy of a person with first chakra issues, sometimes this chakra will appear enlarged and inflamed. It is associated with issues of security and safety, including home, food, shelter, clan and identity.

The second chakra is our center for sexuality, career choice and creativity. The energy of the second chakra is divided into polarities, yin and yang, male and female. It is also where cause and effect take place and where we can create matter out of energy. The second chakra has volatile energy that fuels our motivation around our choices. It also houses the energy of partnership, integrity and honoring one another. When reading a second chakra, look for whether the energy is flowing or appears stagnant. This could relate to issues of abundance, creativity and relationship.

The third chakra is where our will, personal power and intuition resides, which is our soul's way of communicating with our mind. The third chakra, or solar plexus area of our body, is one of the best ways to help us discern the truth. Our solar plexus is open and receiving when there is positive energy, but closes or sends out a blast of energy when harmful people or things are near. The term, 'go with your gut instinct,' I believe, derives from this chakra's capacity of discernment. Energy from people, places and spirits around us are received through the third chakra, move through the central nervous system, and are finally interpreted by our brain.

Domination, power and control are some of the issues that come up in the third chakra for healing. If there is a belief that tells us that we are *less* in some way, we may compensate for this negative message by creating another pattern of belief that says we are *more* in some way.

For example, if a child is taught that he or she is not very smart, it creates an 'I am less than' belief pattern. Then the child wants to compensate to be 'more than,' in order to counterbalance the 'less-than' message that is so deeply ingrained. Going to college and getting a degree, whether or not there is a passion for the subject, may be over-compensating. It also could be a healing step to counterbalance the earlier message and may help that person achieve an authentic life.

The third chakra needs to be cleared, healed and transmuted into the higher frequency of trust, acceptance, and love before we are able to interpret the information, understand the symbols, and transmit the messages from our Spirit Guides, Angels and Ascended Master Teachers. When we are able to show up and leave our egos at the door, and do what we need to from a space of non-judgment, then the connection between the third solar plexus chakra and the fourth heart chakra can be achieved.

Our heart, or fourth chakra, can detect what kind of frequency or type of awareness a wave of energy carries. Only by engaging with the heart, surrendering to Spirit and the greater good, are we able to see things the way they truly are and relay them the way they are intended. A healthy heart chakra appears open. A closed heart chakra may indicate someone protecting their heart, or healing a broken heart.

The fifth chakra, located in the throat area, is the first chakra that focuses primarily on the spiritual plane. The heart chakra is like a bridge and the throat chakra is the crossroads to higher communication. It is the link for our inner and outer worlds. Through this chakra we connect to the Akashic records where we are able to look at past life records, present life lessons or determine future possibilities. The fifth chakra can be used as a portal to bring Source energy into the physical realm, by using sound to voice our own unique expression of Spirit.

When we are in fear or pain we hold our breath, clench our jaw, constrict our throat or even cry out. When we are happy our throats open up, we breathe deeply and make joyful sounds. This chakra is our vehicle for manifestation, or speaking our selves into being. This is why affirmations work so well, and why the voices of the Gregorian Monks or voices in prayer can create an energy vortex with their chanting. It is through the fifth chakra that we speak our truth.

The sixth chakra is what is commonly referred to as the third eye. It is located in the forehead, and can be deceptive if we are not careful with our interpretations. This chakra breaks energy into images, light, color and symbols with emotion. It starts by understanding our personal symbols and what they mean to us, until we trust what we are receiving. The messages can be symbolic or literal. When I do readings, occasionally I am given what seems like movie snippets of my own past that I am meant to share with my client. When I share these stories with them, it is just what they need to hear to make sense of their own personal situation. It is vital to feel the truth or level of awareness in our hearts, otherwise we can be easily tricked with the mirror effects or projections of the third eye.

The crown or seventh chakra has the ability to receive and perceive information straight from Spirit. Some of the things that may need to be healed in the crown chakra are breaks in trust with Source, blocks that may have been placed there when we were children, as a result of parent's personal or religious beliefs, or a head injury from this lifetime or a past lifetime. If our frontal lobes have damage it may also keep us from using our imagination to manifest our desires. When our crown chakra is cleared and healed, we can obtain truth directly from Spirit and see the world around us as it truly is.

The **Eighth Chakra** is located on the back top of the head, merging with the back of the third eye and below the edge of the crown, and it emanates a clear amethyst purple color. For many people, it has just recently become visible and is still becoming a functional chakra. It is increasing in importance, enough to be included in this discussion of the major chakras. Through this chakra, we receive information from our higher selves, Spirit Guides, Angels and Ascended Master Teachers. As this chakra merges with the back of our third eye chakra, we receive our psychic pictures and messages in the brain where they are projected onto our mental screens, the frontal lobes, like a movie. Imagine a movie projector that transfers and interprets input from our third eye, translating language and meaning from other dimensions and converting them to images, sounds and messages in our minds and bodies. The need for this chakra has developed as a result of the spiritual awakening of present times.

We are accessing the previously unused areas of our brains and as a result, have also activated dormant chakras in our auric fields. All the chakras interact together as a system, and affect how we live our lives. By going into a meditative state, we can connect with our higher selves and Spirit Guides. This gives us the ability to see the different layers of activity and to discern what is real and what is imagined. We are able to channel more of our soul's truth than ever before. This allows us to clearly see our way, so that we may be of true service to Spirit.

CHAPTER THIRTEEN

Service to Spirit

"When your consciousness is released from limitation, more of your your psychic abilities become available to you, which are best used in service to Spirit."
~Master Mary Magdalene

When we have done the internal work to awaken to our authentic selves, retrieved and reassembled our soul's purpose, and learned to recognize and live in our heart's truth, we can then fully access our intuitive and healing gifts. In addition, everyone can benefit by assembling their own team of Spirit Guides, Angels, and Ascended Master Teachers whom they trust. And finally, true evolution can only occur when we have handed our ego desires over in service to Spirit.

Sometimes our Spirit Guides have qualities they wish to share with us, and their consciousness can act as a catalyst for bringing forth those abilities. What they share is not always what our ego wants, but it is usually what is needed in our life.

I have observed that our Guides enjoy working with us on earthly projects like community gardening, painting a mural, or opening a center dedicated to helping others. This is a medium for Spirit's energy to grace the physical plane. There are also Archangels, Goddesses, Devas and Fairies who we may connect to. They love personal interaction and are waiting to be asked to co-create with us.

One of the services I offer for clients is clearing spirit activity on a piece of land or property. This is an example of the need for multidimensional healing. Quite often, there is more than one source of activity that requires healing. Imprints from events, cultures, individual people and inter-dimensional beings are left behind as a residue on an area.

Just like people, the land has physical, mental, emotional and spiritual subtle bodies and other energy systems. Like a physical body, the planet's water, rivers and oceans are akin to the planet's blood and circulatory systems. Energy vortexes on our planet can be compared to the body's chakras, the planet's nodes to acupuncture points, the atmosphere to the etheric body of the aura. Ley lines of the planet are very much like meridians of a human body. All things are constructed in this way.

I have a contract with *My Team* to always follow Divine guidance without question. I know that by doing this, I will always be taken care of. This means I'll have a roof over my head, food to eat and my bills will get paid. This agreement has been in effect since I opened Amethyst Healing Center and made my healing work a priority. Since then, *My Team* has always held up their end of the deal.

I once stayed on a piece of land near a client's home. In the process of my work, I met a new Spirit Guide, Ascended Master Teacher Djwhal Khul, and was informed by him that I needed to heal the land and create a vortex for connecting to Spirit on the property. He gave me instructions on how to make what I now know is referred to as a medicine wheel. In the beginning, I had no idea what it was or what it meant. I felt it was his way of connecting with me and providing a space where I could go to meditate and contact him. At first, I was a bit irritated that I was expected to lift rocks, plant shrubs and landscape the area. In the end, it evolved into a very special place for me and remains a lifetime memorable experience that still graces the land.

One of the ways I am of service, is when I'm in meditation asking for healing for my students and clients, to include healing for the planet at this time as well. At other times I ask that my work for the day be dedicated to everyone who needs healing around the world or when I work with a client with a specific issue, that the work I do with them is for all in need of that kind of healing.

One morning I was awakened early by *My Team*. They told me that I needed to start my morning walk earlier than usual. A friend of mine, who I walked with daily, was a little groggy when I woke him up before dawn, but also understood that when I get the calling, we need to be ready to go. We rushed down to the cliffs and I sat on my favorite bench, where I was told to focus on the ocean. I sat there until after sunrise, sending healing energy out to the sea. When I felt my work was done, we finished our walk and headed back to where we had parked. I noticed that we were alone on the path. There was a group of locals who regularly walked the path at the same time every morning, but on this day they were nowhere to be seen. When we got near the entrance, firefighters had placed caution tape across it, and there were several emergency vehicles parked there. A small crowd had formed at the entrance and they were calling to us to hurry up and get out of there. We were told that there had been an earthquake and tsunami in Japan and everyone was waiting for the aftermath wave to hit our coast. Safety authorities had closed the beach accesses to the public. Since I do not watch television, read the newspapers, or listen to the radio, I was not aware that this had occurred. When the tsunami arrived, the waves were larger than normal, but there was no damage to the coastline or our town.

Occasionally, I will get interrupted during a session by one of my Guides with a request that my help is needed somewhere else. This usually means that something requires attention on the frequency that I'm working on. All light workers that are at the same frequency and are in contract with the Ascended Master Teachers are available to be called upon to assist during times of need.

One of my students was with her mother in Kentucky, who was extremely ill and in a coma. I was invited to offer input to the doctors' efforts to help the patient and her condition. At one point her pulmonary specialist called me. The woman's strength was diminishing, and time was of the essence. There were a series of tests that could be given; however, they would all take precious time and drain her energy. I was able to empathically take on her symptoms and tell the doctor what was happening in her body. As a result of this information, he administered the correct tests and she was able to be taken off of life support. I was on the phone as they did this, supporting her with my healing energy. Years later, in her seventh decade, she is thriving and opened a shop as a new adventure.

A few years ago I received guidance from *My Team* that I would be taking a pilgrimage, not really knowing what that actually meant. I even mentioned it to a friend, but told him I did not know where it would be. I assumed that I would be headed to a country in need of healing from war, famine or disease. The very next day I received an email from author, filmmaker and musician James Twyman, also known as the Peace Troubadour. The subject line included an invitation to join him on a 'Pilgrimage to walk the Camino of Saint Francis.' With the use of the word pilgrimage, I instantly knew this was my assignment.

In October of that year I became a member of a forty-person

team blessed to walk in the footsteps of Saint Francis of Assisi. I recognized that my task as a participant would be clearing the painful, martyr energy that accompanied this spiritual path, as well as clearing the land of the accumulation of old stuck energy from beliefs that no longer serve humanity.

I had my assignment, but I wasn't sure how I was going to pay for the trip or manage my regular bills for the month while I was away. I decided not to worry about it and put my faith in *My Team*, who said, *"Stay focused on your work and we will handle the rest."*

The initial monetary deposit, which was required to reserve my spot on the trip, was due only a couple days after I received the email. Much to my surprise, just hours before the deposit was due, a client paid me in advance for an unexpected healing intensive program. It was the exact amount I needed for the deposit! I ended up reserving the last available spot on the trip.

One of my students suggested that, since I was planning to do planetary healing, why not offer to include healing for my clients, students and others? So I sent out an email asking for sponsors and donations, in exchange for adding their consciousness and intentions to my work, while on my pilgrimage. I invited them to send me a note with their prayers and requests for any healing work they would like done for themselves or their loved ones. I carried these with me to Italy.

I flew to Rome, and then took a bus to La Verna, where I spent my first two nights in an active Catholic monastery. Luckily for me, they miscounted our number and I had to be placed in a tiny room in a separate wing, away from everyone else in our group. It just so happened it was the wing where the monks lived. I will never forget the sound of their prayers and chanting as they flowed through the walls of my room and lulled me to sleep.

The next day I toured The Chapel of the Magdalena, built by Saint Francis to honor Mary Magdalene and the sacred feminine.

While in the chapel, I meditated and received instruction to collect holy water from there. This was the beginning of my assignment to collect water from all the shrines and chapels we visited that honored Divine feminine. It was not until I returned home that I learned what I was destined to do with this holy water.

We walked approximately twenty miles a day, from La Verna to Assisi, about two hundred miles, singing, chanting, and in my case, blessing and healing the land. I concentrated on the healing requests of my financial sponsors, and seeded their prayers into Mother Earth with every step that I took.

We arrived in Assisi to attend the twenty-fifth anniversary of the 1986 World Day of Prayer For Peace, when Pope John Paul II had brought together the leaders of the major religions to pray for world peace in their native tongues. On this trip James Twyman filmed a documentary called '*The Camino of Saint Francis,*' which followed the story of Pope Benedict XVI's invitation to religious leaders to again be present on the twenty-fifth anniversary. However, Pope Benedict denied them the right to pray according to their religious practices, limiting the prayers to those of Catholics only. James had taken the original prayers recorded in 1986 and put them to music. He sang these prayers at a concert in Assisi, so that they would still be heard.

While walking the Camino, all of the participants became aware that our group represented every continent on earth. In January, almost three months after I returned home, I received a message that came to me as a letter channeled from *My Team* that the water I had collected was to be sent to my fellow walkers. The blessed waters of the Divine Feminine were to be redistributed on the planet at the Spring Equinox. In essence, the letter revealed to me that the members of our group were being used as channels to create a planetary healing grid by placing the sacred water on every continent. This grid would form multidimensional shafts or columns, energetically connecting the spiritual to the physical. Here is the message they gave me, which I wrote down as I received it:

"The collections of waters and the leaving of waters created anchors for communication and travel, providing a grid that will now be established for your use in dream-time. Your personal agenda with us was to clear old energy and channel the true essence of Us, the Masters, who are worshipped on your planet. True pockets of space were created for our essence to come through, especially in the places of worship. Mass consciousness creates thought forms of who and what we are believed to be. Dogma, pain and martyr energies block or cloud our true essence from being absorbed by the people and the planet. You are creating these shafts just as Yeshua blazed a path from physical to spiritual. This connection is required so that we may all evolve together, gently."

I believe I was chosen to go to Italy by *My Team* for the Peace Conference because the dogma, pain and martyr energies of the world's religious doctrines were assembled there at that time. It was important to go where these energies were thickest, because they served as a catalyst in creating the power points of the planetary healing grid to promote world peace. I believe this energetic healing grid was needed to assist our planet in preparing for the dimensional shifts we are currently experiencing. From this perspective, I know that no part of my trip was a coincidence.

I use the energetic healing grid that I co-created on a daily basis for healing myself, others, and the planet. I especially focus on specific places where there have been or are about to be natural disasters, such as earthquakes, or other growing pains Mother Earth is experiencing. As a result of my experience in Italy, I believe that one of my next assignments will be working with Master Mary Magdalene's Divine feminine essence. I'm just waiting for orders from *My Team*.

CHAPTER FOURTEEN

Creating The Life We Desire

"Creation is a natural state of being. You are consistently creating your moment to moment existence. Co-creating with the Divine Spirit gives you the opportunity to change, heal and expand, so that your life becomes a sacred playground."
~Master Saint Germain

When we live authentically, in the flow, creating the life we are intended to live, the world becomes a serendipitous and magical place. We then can share our passion for life with others and be co-creators of the new paradigm, which is *Heaven and Earth*.

Once we have done the work to live our lives as authentic beings, we can generate the lives we desire from a healthy perspective. We are creating and manifesting our realities every moment of every day, yet most of us have trouble remembering the process. Some of us have spent lives in other existences where things were easily created, yet now, here in this much denser dimension, we find ourselves to be explorers of creation at the most basic and elementary level.

Creating the life we desire is simple, in the sense that we create what we focus on. When we add our emotions to the mix, they act as fuel for our intentions. We draw to ourselves what we love, desire or are focused on. In the same fashion, we repel what we have no attachment to. It is Universal Law that we get back what we send out, or that we draw to us things that vibrate to the frequency we hold most often.

I believe that many of us have had, at one time or another, experienced wanting something that we were so focused on that we were not willing to let it go on any level. It could have been when we were children, not yet tainted by psychological blocks created by those around us. We may have talked about it, fantasized about having it, and made plans about what we would do when we received it, to the point that it never occurred to us that there could have been a possibility that we might *not* receive it. And then it appeared. This is manifestation and creation from our authentic selves. That part of us that is child-like, or has beginner's mind, believed all things were possible, and so they were.

I use this example of authentic manifestation often when working with clients: When we place our order in a restaurant for fish, we do not normally sit and worry that pork will arrive instead. We do not go back and make sure the cook is not preparing pork or remind the waiter that fish is what we ordered. We don't start wondering what we will do if the waiter arrives with the wrong dish. Pretty much, we just trust that fish will arrive because that is what we ordered. In the same way, when we meditate or ask for something that we genuinely desire, ask as if we are ordering that fish. Worry is a waste of our imagination and reroutes our focus onto fearful thoughts and negative images, pushing away what we really want. When our fear overrides our trust, more than likely, the undesired outcome may then appear.

Our karma, belief systems and emotions may block our evolutionary process such that we continue to recreate past experiences over and over again until they are examined and healed. It is like a track that our subconscious mind runs our soul's energy through, repetitively, until it is cleared on all levels. If we give up before the process is complete, we may settle for a life that is not entirely what we desire.

An important precurser to enlightened creating is being thorough with our healing on all levels so that we have a blank canvas on which to create. As we grow and become more powerful, if we are not meticulous in our clearing, we will masterfully replicate our past. This is why sometimes our lessons seem to get more difficult right before we have that 'A-ha' moment or breakthrough experience, and realize we are able to choose differently the next time.

After her marriage ended, Judy thought that by going on a yoga retreat, buying a new wardrobe and getting validation from her girlfriends, that she was ready to start dating again. She was surprised to discover that she attracted the same type of person, in a different body. He looked like a completely different person, but it was still the same energy masquerading as new. As Judy reviewed her life experience, she realized that type of person had been in her life as long as she could remember. Realizing this led Judy to an 'A-ha' moment, and she knew she had to go deeper in her healing process.

Once we are clear of our non-serving programs and belief systems, we can begin to manifest from a position of clarity. Being really clear about what it is you desire is the next step. Sometimes this can be more perplexing than the healing. We do not want to leave our creations to chance or have them be what someone else desires for us. If you want to buy a car, saying, "I want to buy a car" is simply not an adequate request. It aligns you with the energy of wanting not having. Like me, you may be thinking about a deep plum, current model 4-door hybrid sports utility vehicle, with gray interior and fully loaded. But if you are not specific with your request, what may arrive is a 1955 classic truck. The Universal request line has many options. It does not mind if we ask for what we would like in great detail. We need to ask in order to receive, and if we are having trouble with the asking, then it is likely that more effort is needed to clarify our goals.

When we do not exactly know what we want, we can use our imagination and senses to help us. Vision boards, wish lists and visualization techniques are useful and beneficial tools for many of us. They are a form of creating from our authentic, multidimensional selves. These methods may not help us move through and heal the emotional, mental or spiritual obstacles or blocks that have been put in place due to our past life experiences, but they do help us discern what we want. They provide clues that often lead us to heal our pasts.

Meditate and imagine your perfect job, a relationship with your twin flame, or living in your dream home. How do you feel, what do you see, what are you hearing, smelling, or tasting? How are you reacting on a spiritual, emotional or physical level? Speak it into being by talking as if these things are already here, and be openly excited with anticipation of them being on their way. This allows the mind to dial in to the proper frequency of manifestation, to get in alignment with what you desire. It is a compelling way to bring your creative imaginings into the physical realm.

We can use our mental pictures and emotions to fuel our desires. Going back to the example of the car, add the feeling of the steering wheel in your hands, the new car smell, the brilliance of the colors, and how you feel driving it. Make that vision board, journal about your ideas, meditate on your dreams, share your hopes with all your senses and talk about it with all the people who support you.

Include your Spirit Guides, Angels and Ascended Master

Teachers in your creative planning. They can only help if we ask for their help. They allow us to lead, and will not interfere with the process. They assist us with unclear or conflicted messages. They can help us with the healing, and support our decision to be clear of the struggle. Our Divine co-creators empower and amplify our intentions with their energy when it is the in the highest and best intentions for all involved. This will insure that your desires are ones that will support your soul in its advancement.

We do not always know what we want or need, and we may not trust our choices. This is where I suggest that you take time to meditate, and be conscious of what you are asking the Universe to co-create. Sometimes our own ideas are too limited. Asking our Spirit Guides for assistance may bring us rewards beyond anything we could imagine. This allows Spirit's Grace to assist us. Watch for signs to appear giving you information on what your next tasks are. Creating a list of the next steps to take in the process is a great strategy. What are the steps needed to buy that purple sports utility vehicle? If we list them, then we will recognize them as they appear.

Be pure of heart and mind, and have faith that our creations are manifesting. Every day we put our soul's energy toward reaching our goals through meditating, journaling, positive thoughts and words. Be in love with what you are creating. Love is the most powerful emotion available to harness the power of our higher purpose or what is highest and best. Be filled with passion and anticipation at the thought of the outcome and the gift of satisfaction that will accompany your success. Love and positive emotions fuel the birthing of our desired creations. Things are bound to come up that are not in agreement with our intentions. These are signs that help keep us on track. Observe where they are coming from and systematically release, clear and heal those areas. Believe that the Universe takes notice. If we can imagine it, we can make it happen.

On occasion, the universe will hand us something that we may not have asked for, that we may need to take some time to consider or meditate on. It may be part of the bigger plan that we did not see earlier. Sit with it and see how you resonate with this unexpected offering. If for some reason it does not work out, then Spirit has another plan that may be better for us on our path. It may even be something that we put into our blueprint before coming in this life to learn, and our new desires have put us off track. If your intention is for the highest and best outcome for all, trust that the Universe will work with you to create a win win situation, even if it does not feel that way to begin with. Trust that Source will provide what is highest and best on your journey, if you allow it.

One of my clients, Joy, was at a turning point in her life, and she asked for my help to move forward. She had been dating a man who she considered the love of her life. He had led her to believe he was divorcing his wife, and was ready for a new relationship. After more than a year of dating, he decided to give his marriage another chance and their relationship ended abruptly. Their mutual friends grappled with deciding who to support and how to process this change in Joy's status. The majority chose to support the man's return to his marriage, casting Joy in the role of the other woman. Not only did she lose her primary relationship, she also lost friendships that had become important to her personal support system.

Joy's ex-husband had recently moved his new lady friend and her children into his house. The change in family structure affected their son, during their custody visits, who had to deal with sharing his father with his girlfriend and her children. Not surprisingly, he began having difficulties in school, both academically and socially. Joy also had safety and adequacy issues with the apartment where she lived, and was in conflict with her other family members. Even her job became stressful, due to mutual acquaintances connected with her break-up. In short, she felt that nothing in her life was flowing smoothly and she was feeling immense stress.

When Joy came to see me, she wanted to shift every area of her life for the better. The first task I gave her was to make what I call a laundry list. This is a list of all the issues that need attention or adjustment in our lives. As she wrote down these different scenarios, she began to see repetitive themes and patterns. Since she worked in the self-improvement industry, she approached the challenge with a 'workout boot camp' attitude, with me filling the role of coach. She became an excellent student, completing all homework with regularity and eager for the next challenge. She was so ready to get out of all the negative, unhappy situations in her life that many physical or psychological barriers, which are sometimes present when people start this kind of creative work, were absent.

By the time our twelve sessions were over, Joy had literally turned her life around and redirected her energy into her dream existence. She acquired a fantasy home, swimming pool included. This was achieved with the help from a previously non-cooperative family. She and her ex-husband made agreements on how they would raise their son. Subsequently, her son got help and gained the security he needed. His grades came up, and he developed new friendships at school and with his father's new family. Joy earned a raise and promotion at work, with an added bonus of rekindling the friendships that had been lost when her relationship ended. The crème de la crème was when she won a triathlon while overcoming a fear of swimming in the ocean. She confided to me that the traumatic ending of her relationship, which had been the pivotal event that led her to seek me out, had healed, and she was in a new, healthy, committed relationship.

Joy's story is not typical of the usual process of creating the life we desire. I do not want to imply that everyone can heal with such speed and zest as Joy did. Most of the people I see hit psychological or emotional walls or plateaus in their healing process, and may require more time to address their issues. We may know what we need to do to achieve our goals, but may be unwilling to take the actions necessary to make them happen. Integration of our self-knowledge hinges upon application of it into our lives. We each achieve the creation of what is highest and best for us in our own personal, Divine timing. Joy *is* a wonderful example of what we can do if we are ready and willing. She was truly inspiring and confirming for me to work with, and I loved watching her progression unfold in such a successful manner. To stand at the finish line and watch someone take these tools and create the life they desire and deserve to have, is a premium spiritual experience. It has generated positive energy in my life as a teacher.

By the time Amethyst Healing Center had expanded to include several additional practitioners, I was growing in leaps and bounds with my healing practice. One day a woman walked in and asked for an extended healing session. I could see that she was in pain and struggling with physical difficulties. Little did I know that it was another turning point in my personal growth process.

As Karen settled onto the table, and readied herself for our session, we started the standard exchange of background information. She had not even gotten to the point of telling me what her physical ailments were when I noticed that the room was full of spiritual beings surrounding us. Several of my Masters Teachers were present, but there were others who were unknown to me. My instructions from Master Saint Germain were to do as they told me and that all would be fine. After that, I can only compare the healing session to the atmosphere of an emergency room in crisis mode.

I was instructed to give a verbal description of what was happening to Karen, and she seemed to understand what it meant. All she kept saying was, "Get it out of me! Don't stop!" I was given instructions to remove certain symbolic items from her etheric body. I pulled a rose vine with thorns from her chest that I handed to Archangel Michael. As I did this, her physical body would rise and fall, in rhythm with the work. I remember being amazed that she responded in such a manner.

One particular entity seemed to be in charge. He wore a white turban with a turquoise stone on it. His skin was dark and he had piercing hazel eyes. He shouted orders to the others, including me. He actually came into my hands and worked through me, using my body like a bio-suit to do his work.

When the session came to an end, the turban-clad being spoke through me to Karen. He consoled her, telling her that everything would be all right. I remember my voice sounding low, and the words were foreign to me, but the client and the spirit being both seemed to get great meaning from them. I felt as though they were two old friends who had not had the opportunity to speak with each other for a long time, and I was a part of a precious reunion. He had me place my arm under her head as we talked. This is something that I would not have done on my own, but he was in control of my body at the time.

After we finished, I stepped out of the room and sat down on the couch in the entry area. She finally came into the lobby and finished putting on her shoes. She turned to me and asked, "How long have you been doing psychic surgery?" I was not familiar with the term at that time.

I laughed and responded, "About two hours–since you walked in." She was shocked and said she thought I was experienced with this kind of work. I assured her that what had just happened was an expanded version of my previous healing experiences.

She booked another appointment for the next day. She was moving in a couple days and wanted as much help as possible before leaving. That night, my sleep and dreams were extremely active. There were non-stop spirit meetings and conversations. I woke up with Saint Germain's message to me that whatever she asked from me, I was to accept and participate.

The next day's session was still intense but some of the urgency and drama were gone. I was amazed by the clarity of how the spirit beings looked. I was able to notice and observe more details. They also began speaking directly to me instead of treating me as if I was not really there. At the end of the healing session, she came out and told me she had an offer for me. I remember smiling at her and saying, "Yes." She laughed and said, "But I haven't said anything yet!" I let her know that I had been advised by my Master Teacher to accept.

After this, she explained that she had been a healer but had not worked in some time, due to physical limitations. She had congestive heart failure, was diabetic and extremely overweight. She was also on heavy medication. She affirmed the feeling that I had in the first session that there had been sort of a reunion between her and the spiritual entity, who she now identified as Ascended Master Djwhal Khul. With tears streaming down her face, she told me that she had not been able to communicate with him or any other Spirit Guides for years. Thinking that she was under some form of psychic attack and had been excommunicated from her team, she had lost all of her abilities. Her session with me was the first contact to the ethereal realm in years, and she felt that I was the bridge.

She requested that I come to her new home after she had settled in and personally work with her as her private healer for a month. She made the offer financially feasible for me. Based on the guidance I received from Master Saint Germain, I knew I had to agree and trust that the Universe would take care of me. I turned the Amethyst Healing Center over to a woman who was working there, and bought an older model motor home for the journey, which I nicknamed my Gypsy Wagon. I drove to Mount

Shasta, where Karen was receiving healing work from others.

On the night I arrived in Mount Shasta, I began to get huge downloads of channeled information from both her Master Teachers and my own. They were creating a plan or strategy for her. I found myself keeping a journal of this channeled information on the new laptop computer I had just purchased. The information continued to flow into me, and it formed the foundation of this book. I ended up working with Karen in her new home in Oregon for more than two months. When I returned home from that journey, I felt as if I arrived with a confirmation of what my abilities truly were. From my earliest childhood memories, through the pivotal near-death experience with the birth of my first child, my divorce, the loss of my parents, and all the decisions to change my lifestyle, these experiences had taken on a deeper meaning. *The Way* had been illuminated for me.

When I left Oregon, I had concerns that I might not be able to keep up my newly developed, increased energy level. While there, I had time to meditate six hours a day and focus all of my intent upon receiving and understanding information. There were no outside distractions to take me out of that higher dimension of awareness. I was pleased that I was able to preserve my powerful connection to Spirit by making certain adjustments to my environment, and continued to practice daily meditation. To my surprise, I have not only been able to maintain the intensity of my work, it has actually increased. Master Djwhal Khul has been with me since that experience, and is now a valuable part of my healing team. Once again, I am reminded that when I follow Divine guidance, the people, places and things I need show up to support all that I desire to do.

For me, the process of creating the life I desired is exemplified through my story of the process I went through to get to the opening of Amethyst Healing Center. The first day that my door officially opened, I arrived to find the main street blocked off. I inquired as to why this was and someone told me that there was a parade planned for the day. I smile as I remember my reaction to this news. I was elated that someone was throwing *me* a parade! How nice! And, of course, our yearly anniversaries have all subsequently been celebrated by a parade. I have chosen to look at this as a sign that what I am doing is a gift that is to be celebrated, and also to remind myself that I could not have planned it any better. In fact, the enchantment of Amethyst Healing Center is still present today.

This process of believing in my Spirit Guides, Angels, Ascended Master Teachers and most of all, my mastery of self, has revealed the magnitude of what we can accomplish in this partnership, and has escalated through the years. The blessing of this augmentation has been profound, and has brought in expanded calls to service as a multidimensional healer.

I have the faith to know that whatever I do, I will be following the path my soul has designed for me. Every time I can be of service to another, I feel enriched and have validation that I am here with a purpose.

I believe we all won a ticket to ride on this expedition called life. Give yourself permission to receive all that you desire along the way. Realize and unleash your powers of creation, becoming the awakened architect of your life.

"Darkness is simply the absence of light.
Transcend darkness by becoming the light.
May Spirits light shine brightly in you."
~Archangel Michael

Other Titles by The Author

The Art of Awakening is a workbook with exercises and activities, which may be useful to those interested in taking the next step in exploring their intuitive abilities. It can be used by individuals or as part of a class or workshop.

Meditation is an essential aspect to developing our healing and intuitive abilities. ***Dream Awake*** is an enchanting guided meditation book.

For more information please check Darcy's website at: www.DarcyCleome.com

About The Author

Darcy Cleome is a multidimensional healer, spiritual teacher, author and founder of Amethyst Healing Center. She and her dog Chloe live in a quaint artist's village on the central coast of California.

Darcy teaches and lectures internationally, has written books and articles for newspapers and magazines, and has clients all over the world. She works directly with Mother Earth to cleanse, heal, repair and ease the symptoms of our planetary transitions. Darcy has helped many people gain discernment and understanding about their physical, emotional, mental and spiritual health.

Darcy's background and healing modalities include aromatherapy, massage, bodywork, sound healing, guided meditation, journeying, crystal healing, medical intuition, channeling, clairvoyant energy healing and other transformational technologies.

Darcy's goal is to empower her readers, students, and clients in a compassionate and loving way. She assists them in realizing their unique abilities to create lives where they can be their most authentic selves. Everyone has the potential to create the life they desire by practicing *The Way of the Awakened*.

Visit Darcy at her website: www.DarcyCleome.com

INDEX

Akashic	86
Angel	112
Archangel	112
Ascend	105
Ascended Master	105
Aura	70
Chakra	74
Channel	86
Clairaudience	121
Claircognizance	121
Clairgustance	121
Clairessence	121
Clairsentience	121
Clairvoyance	121
Consciousness	53
Gleaning	27
Grounding Cord	78
Hara Line	74
Karma	81
Kundalini	79
Master	105
Matrix	79
Meridians	78
Multidimensional Healing	57
Phenomenon	3
Spirit	52
Soul	49
Source	49
Source Connection	74
Subtle Bodies	71
The Way	93
Transformation	47
Truth	122
Way Seer	119

Recommended Reading

Bailey, Alice A.
Esoteric Healing.
New York: Lucis Publishing, 1953.

Brennan, Barbara Ann.
Hands of Light: *A guide to Healing Through the Human Energy Field.*
New York: Bantam, 1987.

Hay, Louise L.
You Can Heal Your Life.
Santa Monica, California: Hay House, 1982.

Myss, Caroline.
Anatomy of the Spirit.
New York: Three Rivers Press, 1996.

Ruiz, Don Miguel.
The Four Agreements.
San Rafael, California: Amber-Allen Publishing, 1997.

www.ingramcontent.com/pod-product-compliance
Lightning Source LLC
Chambersburg PA
CBHW021956090426
42811CB00001B/53